My Billy Ray Cyrus Story

Some Gave Too Much

My Billy Ray Cyrus Story

Some Gave Too Much

Written by Kari Reeves

Foreword by Del Reeves

Design, typography, and text production:
Maryglenn McCombs

For interviews and other information:
Southern Publishers Group
Birmingham, AL
1-800-628-0903

ISBN: 0-9635026-3-8

Eggman Publishing
2909 Poston Avenue, Suite 203
Nashville, TN 37203

Foreword

by Del Reeves

How do you start a story of one person, like my daughter Kari Reeves, when her resume could exceed seven pages in length?

Kari was born in Modesto, California, on August 1, 1960. Our family moved to Nashville, Tennessee, in 1963. She graduated from high school in Centerville, Tennessee, at Hickman County High School.

After two years at Vanderbilt University in their pre-med/nursing program, she starred in a play called "Oh, What A Lovely War" and loved it so much, she came home and said, "Dad, I think I want to be an actress!"

She started classes at The Acting Studio in Nashville. Kari then went to New York University's School of the Arts to study her craft. She later moved out to California to work under Alan Landers.

Somehow that did not satisfy her and she came back to Nashville to pursue entertaining in the field of country music. She toured all over the world with me and The Good Time Charlies.

After ten years, Kari and I started Del Reeves Productions, Incorporated, where she took on the task of running the company herself. She gave all of her time to trying to make the dreams of others come true - about fifteen different jobs, although she only got paid for one.

I really think that life is like this - you have to do so many different things until you find that one thing that is your niche in life.

One day, our friend Walt Trott, who had the office next to ours in the Country Music Association Building, asked Kari to write for his magazine, *Country Scene*. She had a monthly column called "Kari's Karousel" and wrote feature stories in which she interviewed artists.

I read her interview with John Anderson and thought it was one of the best articles I had ever read. I told her I thought she was missing her niche!

One day, she stopped me as I walked into the office and said, "I have found the artist who will carry on your legacy."

After dragging me over three hundred miles to Huntington, West Virginia, to see Billy Ray Cyrus perform, I said, "Kari, I think you're right."

We both expected Billy Ray to be a huge star. The unexpected occurred the day Billy Ray walked with me to my car and told me that he was in love with my daughter.

All of us want to do the best that we can with our lives. I don't care if you are eighty-five or twenty-five years old, if you are not satisfied with the years you have behind you and don't think that you have created the life you believed in, then you had better get busy! Life is uncertain but has tremendous possibilities and no matter how old you are, or who you are, you have to decide on a goal and work on it.

I believe that is exactly what Kari has done with her writing.

She traveled with us for all of those years and thousands of miles and kept a journal of our escapades—the good times and the bad. I always thought that would be the first book she would write.

Some Gave Too Much is another true-to-life story of living with a star—not just in her work, but in her heart. I wish her the best.

Here's to you, Kari.

———————

Preface

I once heard the saying: "When we experience the rug being pulled out from under us, we must learn to dance on a shifting carpet." While this statement has proved extremely relevant to several different aspects of my life, I feel it is particularly applicable to my Billy Ray Cyrus story.

I have been most fortunate in my life. Not only have I admired the stars in the heavens, but I have walked among stars on Earth. I was born the daughter of Grand Ole Opry star Del Reeves. Thus, most of my youth took place within the realm of country music stardom. I have been honored to share the same stages on tours, special benefit concerts, and in Branson, Missouri with Grand Ole Opry greats. The stars of the Grand Ole Opry were an extension of my family. I loved to sit with Roy Acuff in his dressing room just to be in the mere presence of the King of Country Music. Lorrie Morgan and I grew up trading secrets, gossip, and girl talk backstage. However, I have never known any star in the way I knew Billy Ray Cyrus.

My relationship with Billy Ray seemed a mutual belief in destiny taking its assigned course. I never dreamed that the love we shared would die, but the rug was whisked right out from under my feet.

Now, women all over the world love Billy Ray. They love only the *image* of that hunky, country sensation from Flatwoods, Kentucky.

I fell in love with the real Billy Ray Cyrus - a man who struggled both in his personal life and in his quest for fame. A man whose insecurities and impatience nearly cost him the chance to pursue his dreams. The Billy Ray Cyrus that I loved was a wonderful, caring, sensitive person - a far cry from the macho image he now projects.

I believe that life is a teacher. One of my favorite quotations is "Everything that happens is either a blessing which is also a lesson, or a lesson which is also a blessing." My life with Billy Ray proved to be both. Our relationship served as a difficult lesson in terms of its impact on my heart and my self-respect, but it was a blessing in that it gave me the opportunity to do what I love best, which is to write.

This book, the product of my relationship with Billy Ray, allows the reader admission to the best seat in the house - the theater of my soul and my memories. These are the memories of my time with Billy Ray - time spent enslaved as a consultant, a lover, a friend, as well as a spiritual advisor.

In writing my story, it was in no way my intent to portray Billy Ray Cyrus in an unfavorable light. Nor was it my intent to trivialize the love that we shared. In all honesty, I found it heart-wrenching to have to relive this painful chapter of my life. It is not easy to bare my soul knowing that it may become some entertaining bedside or coffee table gossip. Yet, I have a story to tell and by telling it, it will bring to life the secrets that I hid and the suspicions I ran away from. I'm not hiding or running anymore. I want to tell my story about my life with Billy Ray Cyrus, the little boy with the big dream.

Now, thousands of Kleenex later, I am able to close the book so that you may open it.

I hope you enjoy our dance on the shifting carpet.

———————

Contents

Acknowledgments

I thank God for the gifts.
I thank my Guardian Angels.
"He will give his angels charge of you,
to guard you in all your ways."

I thank St. Jude, the saint of hopeless cases.
I thank St. Anthony, for helping me find what I'd lost.

I thank my family -

My Dad, Del Reeves, for 10 hilarious years on the road and putting me in charge of Del Reeves Productions, Inc., trusting in my judgment of talent, for being a terrific friend and father, making it an honor to be called a Daddy's Girl.

My Mom, Ellen Reeves, for being the foundation that kept a marriage together for 37 years in this crazy business and sacrificing herself for her family. You are my guiding light and the one that could put a band-aid, even on my heart, and make it all better.

Anna Delana, my sister, for being someone I can only hope to be but never will. You are a rare bird in a gilded cage and soon the world will hear your sweet songs. You are an inspiration!

Bethany, my sister, for uncontrollable laughter through my tears, who was my life buoy when I was drowning in the "deadline sea" and rescued me from May Day. You are my life preserver.

I LOVE YOU ALL!

To Richard Courtney, my publisher, who believed me from the first day when I handed him an idea on three little sheets of paper and said "You're a writer. Now go write."

To the staff at Eggman Publishing, especially Maryglenn, who worked so very hard to make my dream come true.

To Randy Tarkington, thanks for twenty years of watching "Auntie Mame" reruns and harmonizing to every Broadway musical I'd sing, and to all my best friends. I am so fortunate to have you in my life!

To George Owens, one of the longest survivors of my Dad's band, "The Good Time Charlies," who helped me day and night with my computer crises.

To anyone who buys a copy of *Some Gave Too Much* and shares with me, the memory of a time that is forgotten by some, but not forgotten by all.

Chapter 1

The Interview

In 1988, I was working as a freelance journalist for *Entertainment Express* magazine, along with managing my father's company, both of which were based in Nashville, Tennessee, in the heart of the vicinity referred to as Music Row. Music Row is an area comprised of almost a square mile in which the entire Nashville music industry is located. These few streets house the multi-billion dollar music business.

On April twenty-sixth of that year, Scott Faragher of In Concert International, a booking and management company, called me at my office at Del Reeves Productions and inquired if I would be interested in interviewing what he referred to as "the newest country sensation."

Although this was at least the fourth or fifth "newest country sensation" I was given the opportunity to interview on this particular week, I grudgingly agreed. Scott responded that sensation number six would be right over.

Minutes later, I thought I had witnessed pop sensation George Michael strolling through my door. However, this figure introduced himself to me as Billy Ray Cyrus.

My initial reaction to this gorgeous man who had just entered into my territory was the thought that he should have been a model for International Male instead of an aspiring country singer. His eyes immediately locked onto mine and held me at gun point. Miraculously, I managed to ask him to sit down. Even more miraculously, his rear end found its way into a chair. This man was scared to death.

As I scoped this green, frightened sapling, my own eyes noticed his piercing hazel eyes. I also noted he was wearing a pair of beige, suede, fringed, cowboy boots nearly identical to a pair that I owned. He wore tight Levi's tucked inside the boots and a long-sleeved purple shirt, somewhat reminiscent of the sixties. His hair was short on top and shoulder-length in the back.

After a few minutes of polite banter between Scott, Billy Ray, and myself and a few phone interruptions, I noticed Billy Ray still remained nervous. I had never considered myself an intimidating person, and I sometimes forgot that my position with a national country music magazine often made the aspiring singers on edge.

When I sensed that he was comfortable enough for me to begin conducting the interview, I learned the story of Billy Ray's life. As he began to unfold the events of his life leading him to this point in time, my mind wandered from the interview and I imagined him, adorably frocked in a choir robe singing in a Flatwoods, Kentucky, Pentecostal Church.

During our conversation, I learned that sports played a major part in Billy Ray's life throughout high school. Billy Ray was even offered a baseball scholarship to Georgetown College, a small, private, Baptist college in Kentucky, where, interestingly enough, dancing was strictly forbidden until recently. As much as he loved baseball, Billy Ray's desire to be a musician prompted him to reject the offer. Thus, he traded in his baseball bat for a guitar.

Billy Ray formed his first band, The Sly Dogs, shortly thereafter. The band gained such regional popularity that Billy Ray would soon decide that in order to make the big time, he should make the big move to California.

My curiosity got the better of me and I asked him why he had opted for California when Nashville, *the* Music City, was so much closer. Billy Ray explained that he felt that his musical style was too rock and roll for Nashville, in spite of the urgings of his friends in Kentucky. People he talked to in

Nashville suggested he go to California. Ironically, once he arrived in California, people suggested that he try his luck in Nashville. In short, *nobody* wanted anything to do with Billy Ray Cyrus.

Billy Ray's inability to conform or fit into any kind of musical mold haunted him. However, he persevered and continued to make his own musical statement.

Before he gave up on California, he stopped playing music and began dancing to it. Billy Ray began a career as a professional male dancer. His hesitance to discuss the subject intrigued me. When I attempted to delve deeper into this interesting facet of his life by remarking that he must have enjoyed having beautiful women screaming at him, he insisted that he did not and stated that he began to feel sleazy about this career choice.

Billy Ray's uneasy feeling about his new profession soon resulted in his dropping his G-string and picking up a three piece suit, as he accepted a position selling cars in Woodland Hills, a suburb of Hollywood. Although he made nearly $36,000 in six months, he decided to give up the job when he realized that a career in music was more important to him than any sum of money he could make selling cars.

By this point in time, Billy Ray had reached the realization that he could not attain his dream unless he worked at it constantly and abandoned everything but the pursuit of music. He was obsessed with his desire for musical stardom and he refused to stop until he had captured that dream. Billy Ray knew in his heart that he would never be satisfied doing anything else.

He returned home to Huntington, West Virginia, and formed another band, which he dubbed Billy Ray and the Breeze. According to Billy Ray, the band maxed out after about a year of playing together. He seemed to believe that the other band members were in it only for the booze, the women, and the drugs, a shocking discovery in the entertainment business. He, however, claimed to be serious about the music.

In September of 1987, Billy Ray came to Nashville where he met Scott Faragher of In Concert International. Billy Ray soon signed a management and booking contract with Faragher, which entitled Faragher to thirty percent of Billy Ray's earnings.

Under Faragher's guidance, Billy Ray returned home to Kentucky and formed another band, Billy Ray and the Players. From Sly Dogs to Breeze to Players back to the Sly Dogs - gigantic leaps in creativity. The group's repertoire consisted mainly of original material, but often included several Lynyrd Skynyrd tunes and such songs as "Mony, Mony" and "Simply Irresistible." The band soon took Texas, North and South Carolina, as well as the tri-state area - Kentucky, Ohio, and West Virginia - by storm. They decided to expand their touring schedule into more states.

As a general rule, I always asked interview subjects about their personal lives, i.e., marital status, children, etc. My philosophy was that it was interesting to include some personal information about the subjects in my articles for I did not think any one wanted to read only about the business sides of the artists.

I was genuinely interested in Billy Ray's responses to these questions. When asked if he were married, he responded that he had been married for two years. He said his wife, whose name was Cindy, was not overjoyed by his choice to follow his dream.

I could not quite identify the emotion that washed over me when he mentioned his wife. In retrospect, I realize that it must have been disappointment.

I sincerely enjoyed getting to know Billy Ray through the interview. His innocence, coupled with his genuine enthusiasm, was refreshing, especially in a world which often featured phony facsimiles acting out their lives.   In this first meeting, I learned far more about this incredible man than mere facts on which to base my article.   After this one brief meeting, I felt like I *knew* him.

———————

Chapter 2

Similar Beliefs

One thing that struck me in my first meeting with Billy Ray was the similarity between us. It was uncanny. He wore a crystal and a St. Christopher medal on a tarnished silver chain around his neck. I sported my own crystal on a bracelet and carried a St. Jude card and a rosary from Medugorje, the small village in Yugoslavia where the Blessed Virgin Mary appears daily to young school children, in my wallet.

Additionally, Billy Ray and I bonded when we discovered that we were mutual students of Earle Nightingale and Norman Vincent Peale, both positive thinking gurus. He confessed that Earle Nightingale's "Acres of Diamonds" story was one of his favorites. We laughed at not having read *Dianetics* and vowed to read it together someday.

In this, our first meeting, Billy Ray announced that he felt as if he had known me for years. The feeling was mutual.

After my initial encounter with Billy Ray, my younger sister Bethany paid Scott Faragher and Billy Ray a visit at In Concert. She and Scott were friends at that time. Billy Ray told Bethany that I had made quite an impression on him. Bethany would later inform me that Billy Ray had said he had never met anyone so full of life or of energy. While I had decided not to disclose my feelings to anyone, Billy Ray had made quite an impact on me, too.

The following day, my next door neighbor at the Country Music Association Building, Walt Trott, editor of *Country Scene* magazine, told me that Billy Ray had stopped by to visit me. When I heard about his visit, I was, quite frankly, puzzled.   I could not imagine why he had come by to see me.

One week later, on May 3, Billy Ray came into my office and stayed for several hours. As an excuse, he said he wanted to make sure the interview had gone well. This was merely a thin veil to disguise the real reason he had come by. We barely even mentioned the article during our chat. Although I knew that Billy Ray had stopped by purely for personal reasons, I pushed that thought out of my mind, scared to allow myself to think such thoughts.

He was intrigued by the collection of pictures on my wall. When he noticed a photograph of me on stage with Dad, he asked if I was a singer. I jokingly told him that what I lacked in vocal ability, I made up for with my stage presence.   I told him that I had recently recorded a song called "Roll Out the Red Carpet." The song, which was written by Danny Chauvin and Jim Allison, was a brazen, country tune. Chauvin had requested that I record the demonstration, or demo, tape of the song. Because he felt that the song mandated an unconventional, daring interpretation, Danny had chosen to enlist my vocal aid.

Billy Ray sounded genuinely interested in the material, as he too saw himself as unconventional and daring. He wanted to hear my demo, but I explained that the only copy of the song was at my apartment. He suggested that we drive over and get it.

We decided to drive over in the non-descript two-door car he was driving at the time so that he could stop and buy some gasoline since he was almost out of gas. My apartment was located on Belmont Boulevard, near Belmont University, the training ground for a great deal of the talent - both administrative and creative - on Music Row. Although the apartment was in close proximity to my Music Row office, the brief ride over yielded even more remarkable similarities between the two of us.

I came to the conclusion that Billy Ray was as obsessive-compulsive as I when I noticed him triple-check the gas cap on his car before we drove away. He further confirmed my suspicions once he got back in the car when he asked me whether or not I noticed him put it back on. I laughed at his, and at my own, compulsiveness. Through my laughter, I explained to him that I was equally compulsive since I could barely leave my apartment without walking into each room to make sure the lights were out, and triple-checking the coffee pot. Even then, I would have to re-check the door locks before I could leave comfortably. By the time I left, it was time to come home again.

Billy Ray exhibited another of his phobias when he immediately panicked after realizing that a bee had flown into the car. He explained that he had been attacked by a swarm of bees when he was younger, and he still had a terrible fear of them. As we laughed at each other and at ourselves, I could not help but marvel at all of the things Billy Ray and I had in common. Remembering that being unmarried was one thing we unfortunately did not share, I tried to put marital status out of my mind.

Once we arrived at my apartment, Billy Ray amused himself by admiring my collection of clowns in the kitchen. I explained to him that the clowns served as my reminder that I always want to present myself to the world as a happy person. I felt so close to him at that moment that I confided in him about how I had always felt the need to try to make other people around me happy. He told me that he had known another girl who collected clowns, but for a different reason. I noticed that his eyes lingered on mine as he said it.

I could have stayed there for hours, just talking to him and looking into those beautiful eyes, but my better judgment told me that we needed to leave. I grabbed the tape, headed for the car, and back to the office. We popped the demo into the cassette player and listened to my song. Billy Ray said he loved it and asked if he could keep it for his drive back to Ohio. I agreed to give him the demo and assured him that my scream- ing vocals would keep him awake and amused.

Before he dropped me off at the office, his eyes gazed deeply into mine yet again as he told me that he had never met any- one quite like me. Assuming that he intended it to be a com- pliment, I thanked him. As I walked back towards my office, I stole a glance over my shoulder as I watched Billy Ray drive away. I shook my head ever so slightly to rid myself of the thoughts that swarmed around in my head, just like the bees that had once attacked Billy Ray. He would be the object of many attacks in the years to come - both from critics and from fans - attacks of love, hate, jealousy, and rage.

———————

Chapter 3

The Invitation

Thoughts of Billy Ray played upon my mind rather frequently in the days which followed. While I maintained that he and I were involved only in business - which at this point was true - I could not help but remember how he had made me feel such a part of his life.

I put a great deal of effort into my article about Billy Ray and I realized a special sense of satisfaction out of devoting so much time to his cause. I was pleased to have been able to convince my editor, Walt Trott, that we should use the Billy Ray story in the Fan Fair issue of the magazine. This was exceptionally important for our distribution doubled for this issue.

On May 17, Billy Ray called me at the office and I read him the finished article. He was thrilled with it and excited to have been included in the Fan Fair issue. Furthermore, he did not object to the mention of the history of his previous careers, in particular the male dancing. He asked me how I could know him so well. We had a lengthy conversation about the music business and about our company, Del Reeves Productions.

After we had discussed business, Billy Ray mentioned that he had dreamed about me the night before. Naturally, my curiosity was piqued. He told me he dreamed that he was driving to Las Vegas in a blue Corvette to catch a show in which I was the headlining act.

I had gotten into the habit of writing down notes from every phone conversation I ever had. After years of talking to so many different people during the day, I found this to be the easiest way to remember who had said what. When Billy Ray told me about this dream, I was puzzled as to why he was telling me this in the first place and wrote "Ain't that sweet?" in my journal.

I laughed and told him that I thought he had listened to my tape one time too many. He informed me that he had experienced withdrawal symptoms after listening to my song for six hours straight on his trip home. After this, Billy Ray began calling on a weekly basis.

His call on Wednesday, June 22, came as no surprise since, by then, we could have qualified for the frequent caller plan with AT&T. He called to tell me that he would be in Nashville the upcoming weekend playing at a club called the Cuckoo's Nest. Scott had already made me aware of it and I informed Billy Ray that I planned to be there on Saturday night.

Saturday, Scott called and invited me to join him for dinner before the show. Since I was looking at the last can of Campbell's Chicken Noodle soup in my cupboard, I graciously accepted the offer.

He picked me up in one of the convertibles from his rather extensive collection and we headed to downtown Nashville to the San Antonio Taco Company, the city's favorite Tex Mex restaurant. There we dined on soft chicken tacos, nachos with guacamole, and Dos Equis beer. After dinner, Scott dropped me off at my apartment and I followed him to the club.

Upon our arrival, we met the guys in the band. Scott and I were seated and ordered drinks as we awaited Billy Ray's performance. The stage was so small that Billy Ray would have landed in the dancing crowd had he attempted to execute the "Achy Breaky Turn-Around." What impressed me the most that evening was the audience's response to him. His popularity had reached such proportions that he literally had his own following. I met a group of attractive blonde ladies who had driven all the way from West Virginia to the Music City in order to see him perform that night. Obviously, I was not the only blonde who had been stricken with the Cyrus virus!

Following the show, Billy Ray returned to his room at the Shoney's Inn on Music Row and phoned me. We talked until the wee hours of the new day as the sun began to peek through my window shades.

He asked me several times if he could come over to see me. I agreed to allow him to seek solitude because I realized that he needed to take a little time away from the guys in the band and from his fans. I understood how even ardent fans can sometimes become a burden since the star has to be "on" when he is around them. I was the same way on the road with my father all those years trying to be protective of his needs. I knew that Billy Ray lacked the quiet time to regroup his energies.

I offered to let him crash at my place for a couple of hours and promised him that no one, especially me, would bother him. He could become virtually invisible. He responded that he would love to, but voiced the concern that he might have considerable difficulty staying out of trouble.

My reputation was still intact, so I promised to throw holy water on him to cure him of his evils. That offer also served to reinforce my own weak resolve to resist his charms. The weeks of phone calls and weekly visits, along with the feeling that we had known each other in past lives, had led me to question my relationship with Billy Ray. The closeness we felt, his repeated confessions about his unhappy marriage, and our commitment to a life-long friendship were beginning to play Russian Roulette with my mind. I knew that Billy Ray's coming over could have gotten us in, not holy, but *hot* water.

———————

Chapter 4

The First Kiss

On November 2, Billy Ray was performing at a showcase at the Stagedoor Lounge at the Opryland Hotel. The showcase, sponsored by In Concert International, featured another band, Razorback, and Billy Ray and the Players. I was eager to see him perform again.

I met Billy Ray, his lead guitarist Terry Shelton, and his bassist Harold Cole in the hall outside the lounge. Billy Ray seemed a little uptight about his upcoming performance, so I suggested that we take a walk to work off some of his nervous energy.

I recommended to Billy Ray that we go to the conservatory, a peaceful place within the confines of the Hotel that might not be filled with so many hotel dwellers. Being an honorary mascot of the Opry family, I felt qualified to serve as his tour guide through the land of Opry Oz. If he had only had a heart and I had only had a brain!

We were in view of the sky-high golden bird in the golden cage amid countless waterfalls when he climbed up on one of the rocks and turned to me. He held out his hand beckoning me to join him, which I did. He hesitantly asked if he could kiss me. I should have remembered the oath I took backstage at the Opry when I promised my father that I would never mix business with pleasure. I justified it by rationalizing that the article was already in the hands of *Entertainment Express* subscribers and my business was therefore complete. I was no longer involved in Billy Ray's business: I was now his friend, his confidant, spiritual teacher, and sounding board.

I expected the kiss to be a quick peck on the cheek, but it wasn't. His hands and our lips quivered apprehensively as they touched, and our gazes locked onto one another fiercely. The kiss was intense, and the eye contact between us was just as passionate. We both tried to shake off the feeling that the kiss ignited long after we had pulled away from one another. I knew that it was I, and not his upcoming performance, that was making him this nervous.

That night, I received bruised ribs from the elbow of my younger sister Bethany, who continuously poked me while I sat, ever so coolly, at the VIP table in the lounge. Billy Ray sang "I Never Ever Thought I'd Fall In Love With You" as if I were the only person in the room. It must have been obvious for I endured lowered elbows and raised eyebrows from everyone at the table.

———————

Chapter 5

The Bubble Bath

It took nearly seven months after the meeting where I had interviewed Billy Ray for *Entertainment Express* magazine for me to admit to myself just how I felt about him. I guess, just as the song said, I never ever thought I'd fall in love with him. We both concluded that we must have met and loved many times before in previous lifetimes, so what was to stop us from loving in this life? As you can see - absolutely nothing.

Billy Ray called me at the office from Shoney's Inn, Room 115, sounding somewhat dejected, rejected, and neglected by Music Row. He had decided to take a long bath to alleviate some of his tension, but complained that he had no bubble bath. When he called, I was just about ready to turn off my typewriter, hit the lights, and rid myself of my own stress from another productive, yet grueling day on Music Row. The tone of Billy Ray's voice and his plight somewhat expediated my departure. I went to purchase his requested bubble bath and decided to pick up some beer, too.

I spent several minutes in Walgreen's perusing the bubble bath selection. I finally opted for Calgon, deciding that the poor boy really did need to be "taken away."

By the time I arrived, Billy Ray was already out of the bathtub and met me at the door dressed only in a pair of faded blue jeans. His now-famous sleeveless T-shirt was tossed casually across a chair. He looked at me with those big, hazel eyes that I knew had broken plenty of hearts and told me I was beautiful both inside and out. I felt guilty after the compliment because I stood there with only a fifty-nine cent trial size bottle of Calgon, but managed to mutter, "You're welcome."

Billy Ray asked me if I had time to come in. He said he wanted to play me some of the songs he had written. As he retrieved his guitar, I left in search of an ice bucket. Upon entering the bathroom, I found the sink already filled with ice and Bud Light. I crammed my Stroh's Light into the sink.

I don't know why I felt so uneasy. I guess my nervousness stemmed from the fact that this was the first time I had been in a situation with Billy Ray where a bed - not a desk - was the focal point of the room.

Billy Ray sat down on the bed and began to serenade me with the songs that would later comprise his multi-platinum album. I listened attentively to the unplugged, and semi-undressed, versions.

Billy Ray's songs were impressive to say the least, while his guitar playing was good but nothing spectacular. He could play just enough to get by and confessed that he wished he could play better, but I was greatly impressed with his lyrics.

Billy Ray put his guitar aside after a few songs and pulled out his *TNT: The Power Within You* book. He referred to this small, simple, self-help book as his Bible. I confessed that this was the one positive thinking book that I did not own, so we read each other parts of the book and talked about its meaning for hours.

I could have made an exit then and left with my morals and business sense still in place. However, he had asked me to bring him the bubble bath. As he laid on the bed, face-down, and asked for a back massage for about the trillionth time, I succumbed, deciding that I might be able to heal Billy Ray's mind and rub out some of his negative "I hate Nashville" energy in the process. I decided it was the least I could do since his much-desired bubble bath had not happened.

After I had thoroughly massaged every inch of his muscular back, Billy Ray offered to return the favor. I knew that when my Vanderbilt T-shirt got in the way of those strong hands, I still had on three additional coats of armor: a camisole, a bra, and a little voice screaming inside my head.

The T-shirt served its purpose until I was gently rolled over and my neck was kissed lightly. We decided to relinquish the T-shirt since Billy Ray himself was only wearing blue jeans with the top button undone.

Billy Ray's hands slowly slipped the pink, spaghetti straps of my camisole down to my shoulders and I shed yet another layer of my coat of armor. For nearly the next hour, we explored each other intimately but remained in our blue jeans. Those sensuous moves he demonstrated must have been choreographed during his dancing days.

Later, as wrong as it was, I forgot the rosary in my purse and the promise I had made backstage at the Opry. I tried desperately not to remember that this man - this wonderful, beautiful man - was married. After all, he had told me that he had a wife and that he did love her, but he thought that their marriage had been a mistake. He told me that he thought we were soulmates. Soulmates or not, when he removed my blue jeans, I reciprocated. It was then that we discovered yet another similarity between the two of us: neither of us was wearing any underwear.

I continued to ignore the screaming voice in my head as Billy Ray and I began to make love passionately. Afterwards, we were both so emotionally and physically exhausted that we fell asleep in each others' arms.

We awoke to a ferocious thunderstorm long before his 6:00 AM wake-up call. We made love again while the thunderstorm crashed noisily in the world outside his hotel room. The electricity from the storm paled in comparison to the electricity generated by the two of us.

Afterward, I put on my clothes and prepared to leave. Billy Ray offered to walk me out to my Blazer. I walked out of the room with my hair in tangles and my soul no less in disarray. I could not get a brush through my hair for a week and my soul took far longer to recover. Billy Ray picked a red rose that was growing by the poolside, gave it to me, and asked me if it was all right for him to tell me that he loved me.

I had no rose to give him, so I handed him my heart.

———————

Chapter 6

The Martha Washington Inn

Later that November, Billy Ray called to tell me that he would not be returning to Nashville for a couple of weeks because of road dates. It was around the same time I received a letter from Scott Faragher enlisting my help in any way to get Billy Ray on *Nashville Now* or on the television series I was co-directing at the time, which featured established artists and the newcomers. During our conversation, he asked me if I had ever heard of the Martha Washington Inn in Abingdon, Virginia. Being an avid reader of *Southern Living*, I had read articles about it and had always wanted to visit there. When Billy Ray invited me to join him there, I accepted excitedly. I knew I would be stuck with the bill, but it was a small price to pay for the opportunity to spend time with the man who had begun to dominate my thoughts and dreams.

In order to prime him for our rendezvous, I told him the story of Beth, the lovelorn ghost whose morose spirit roams the third floor of the Inn sadly playing her violin. He thought I was kidding, but I insisted that I had not contrived the touching, yet heartbreaking, love story. It was really no wonder that he did not believe me for the story bore such a striking resemblance to our own lives. Beth and her lover, like Billy Ray and myself, were ill-fated lovers who were forbidden to be together. I told him that I thought it would be an appropriate place for us to be together, since we were lovers lost in time, yet it was the present and we wanted to break the haunting spell so our future could be without ghosts of the past.

I prepared for my trip by throwing my Rand McNally map in the front seat and my clothes and cooler in the back. With this minimal preparation, I headed east on Interstate 40.

Billy Ray had asked me to call if I happened to be running late. Since I was behind schedule, I pulled off the road in Knoxville and called the front desk of the Inn as he had requested. He was standing right by the desk in the lobby, anxiously awaiting my call. The sound of his voice caught me by surprise. I had expected to leave a message with the front desk, yet during Billy Ray's band break, he had been hanging out by the phone in case I had called.

When I arrived, Mrs. Washington's three-story, bricked main entrance and her surrounding buildings were breathtaking. The place was especially charming during the holiday season. Tiny white lights danced in the yard like little fairies playing hide and seek with glowing icicles. As I pulled into the curving driveway, I heard the sounds of Billy Ray and his band emanating from the lounge. Colonel Francis Preston, builder of the Inn, had not quite mastered the art of sound-proofing in 1832.

I walked into the magnificent, warm, and historic edifice. Fires burned in the sitting rooms where huge portraits of Miss Martha and her contemporaries kept watch on all who entered. Christmas trees decorated with old-fashioned ribbons and trinkets adorned each room. I left a message at the front desk for Billy Ray giving him my suite number in the garden wing.

The militaristically charming bellman took my pass key and showed me to my suite, then left to retrieve my luggage. He took my suitcase, placed it in the bedroom, and, with a twinkle in his eyes, gingerly sat my $1.99 styrofoam, Jim Dandy cooler down in the sitting room. He then returned with an ice container and ice into which he expertly placed my beer.

The suite itself was beautiful. The sitting room featured a

large desk and chairs, a couch, and some splendid antique pieces. The bedroom sported a magnificent four-poster mahogany bed which rose high up off the ground. Atop the bed were lavishly embroidered lace pillowcases. Huge windows overlooked the garden. Even the bathroom was magnificent!

I knew that Billy Ray had previously made me feel the earth move under my feet, but this time, I literally felt the floor move beneath my feet. The tremor was caused by a bass guitar and a kick drum. Eventually, the sounds of silence invaded. The quiet was interrupted only by the sound of my heart pounding loudly in my ears. I had not laid eyes on Billy Ray since he had picked the rose for me and told me that he loved me. I was so excited to be seeing him again that I temporarily forgot about all the reasons why we should not be together in this not so well-concocted tryst. What would the boys in the band think? I knew we had to get our stories straight and was on the brink of a master plan when the phone rang. It was Billy Ray asking me to let him through the entry not only to my heart, but also to the door that kept him from my suite.

He was as nervously excited as I was. When he kissed me hello, his hands were shaking just like they did that night at the Opryland Hotel when he kissed me for the very first time. His lips were as warm and as sweet as I had remembered and I felt all of my nervousness and apprehension drain away from me. He asked me how I could be standing there looking the way I did. I remarked coyly that I looked the way I did because of the way he made me feel. I didn't bother to mention that I had to spend twenty dollars at the tanning salon to achieve this warm glow.

We went into the sitting room and he tried on my red, fringed jacket that was hanging on the back of a chair. He paraded around the magnificent room in my Avanti jacket with an arrogant flair. We each grabbed a beer and slid onto the couch.

The mood shifted abruptly from romantic to tyrannic as Billy Ray launched into a tirade about how unhappy he was with Scott Faragher. He was dissatisfied because he felt as if the people at In Concert were not getting him enough bookings and that Scott was working harder for his other artists. Since this was not an unusual reaction for artists to have towards their management, I endured his complaints.

Billy Ray suggested that I try to help him in some way. He told me that I was the only one who really believed in him. He hinted that I talk to Dad about representing him.

I was in complete harmony with Billy Ray on this matter. I had witnessed him on-stage and knew what a powerful presence he had as a performer. His enthusiasm prompted him to ask me to retrieve a legal pad so we could write down some of his "selling points" so that I would have plenty of ammunition for my talk with Dad.

His list consisted of five goals we would adopt:

#1 Please always remind me: Always be myself. Always be who I am and what I am. If people like me and respect me for what I am then that is good, for I need people. But...if someone doesn't like me then that is good also for they don't live their lives for me, so why should I live mine for them?

#2 Talk about Scott splitting his management contract with Kari so we can get rockin'. Scott is good at what he does and he can help but he is very busy so Kari could do most of the work and he would be there to do what he does.

#3 Record in January. Record with my guys and some more real talented people from where I live (banjo, steel, acoustic).

#4 All these things will interweave us so tight. We must grow together!!

#5 Regional. I got my own little market. We can start makin' money before a hit record.

We kept talking through the early hours of the morning. At around 4:30, we decided to venture upstairs to the third floor in search of the ghost of Beth. We were caught by a wide-awake bell-boy who seemed extremely bored. He accepted the invitation of showing around two love struck, semi-intoxicated ghost busters and led us on a private tour of the Inn. Billy Ray and I were intrigued by the story and anxious to catch a view of Beth's ghost. We were disappointed that Beth did not appear before us, so we resolved to write our own love story.

I came to bed dressed in a sheer, white night gown that played languidly about my ankles. I floated into the historical bedroom as if I were drifting back in time, to the time I dreamed it was - a time when we were not forbidden to be together. I didn't need Billy Ray to take the gown off of me, but I wanted to give him a vision of the past and of the future. I watched him staring at me intently as I stood at the end of the bed and disrobed slowly. I climbed underneath the covers and lay beside him. We gently took control of each others bodies and minds. We became lost in the moment and drifted even further off into the world where I was allowed to love this man as much as I did.

That night, we added to the repertoire of love stories at the Inn. Now there is my own "Kari Reeves as she remembers the magical evening she shared with her one great love on the second floor in room 210" - story - a story where history once again repeats itself - forbidden lovers forgotten by time.

It was midday when the light greeted us. I immediately called room service for coffee and the front desk for a late checkout. Our one night in that enchanted place seemed like a dream. I hated to leave the security of the Inn for I feared that I could never find comfort in any other place. As I looked around the room - at the bed sheets and mattress cover dangling from the corner of the bed, the bedspread in the middle of the floor, those lace pillows strewn on the bathroom floor - I hoped I would be able to seek comfort again in this five star dwelling.

I got out of bed and started the shower, falling over the havoc on the floor, which matched the havoc raging within my heart. I loved letting the hot water run slowly over my body as I replayed in my mind each precious moment that had recently transpired. While I was at the sink brushing my teeth, Billy Ray joined me in the fog and wrapped his arms around my waist. We quickly moved from the bathroom and headed back underneath the covers that were not there.

———————

Chapter 7

Love Notes

I didn't want to leave Billy Ray and it was obvious that he didn't want to leave me either, but my American Express account was nearing my self-imposed limit, so I regretfully decided to curtail our stay at the Martha Washington Inn. Plus, we had practically destroyed Room 210! I checked out, loaded up my car, and we drove into nearby Bristol, Virginia, to eat Chinese food.

We convinced ourselves that by eating there it would shorten my trip back to Nashville. We both knew that in actuality I would still have to drive him back to the band house in Abingdon after we ate. If we needed any other excuse to prolong parting with one another, we reasoned that the mixture of rain and snow in the forecast could serve that purpose, although we knew it could neither dampen our love nor chill the fires which raged within us.

We were dressed in jeans and looked like we hadn't slept, probably because we hadn't. Billy Ray seemed equally remorseful about our imminent parting. His face showed the sadness which the separation would bring.

In order to get my mind off of what was to come, I looked down at the Chinese Zodiac and read us our horoscopes. Billy Ray's birth year made him the Buffalo. His zodiac said: "You are a born leader. You inspire confidence from all around you. You are conservative, methodical, and good with your hands. Guard against being chauvinistic and always demanding your own way."

I marveled at how aptly this description fit Billy Ray. After watching him on stage, it was apparent that he really was a "born leader." I could certainly attest to the validity of the prophecy that Billy Ray was good with his hands!

Outside, the weather forecast was proving indeed true, so we decided that it was far too dangerous for me to drive home to Nashville due to the fact that the road conditions were steadily worsening. The next exit sign we saw read "Weary Travelers Sleep here" so I pulled into the Comfort Inn. I checked in, feeling that I would be in no less danger on the treacherous roads outside. I knew my heart's condition was worsening along with the roads as I prolonged the inevitability of leaving especially when our past experiences had promised us such a bright future.

Billy Ray came to my room with me as I got settled in. His pretense was that I needed help with my luggage. He asked if we could take a nap because he had a long night ahead of him. We tried to fall asleep after making love, but sleep never came. After minutes, or after an hour, he said my name softly and when I answered, he asked if I could sleep. When I said no, he suggested that we go to Shoney's for coffee.

At Shoney's, we listened to the couple sitting behind us. They had lots of babies and were asking for highchairs and crackers. We talked about having babies of our own. I realized that our communicating and showing each other "I love you" in bed was not nearly as important as the communication we shared in believing in one goal - and that goal was to see him succeed so that we would be together, even if we had to lie and cheat to get it.

I took Billy Ray back to the band house so he could get ready for the show and I went back to the room. After the show, I talked to the guys in the band and complimented them on their performance. Then Billy Ray and I went to the band house to pack up a few of his belongings so he could spend the night with me at the Comfort Inn. In order to justify Billy

Ray's departure, we told his band members that we were going to join my Mom and Dad. We concocted this slight fib in order to quell any suspicions that the band members might have. Even though they were musicians, I doubt they fell for it, but it was worth a try.

We headed back to my room, put a few beers on ice and drank them in bed as we wrote notes to each other. The game started on the back of the grocery bag that I'd brought the beer in.

Billy Ray began by writing:

"When do you know
  if it's false,
When do you know
if it's true. . ."

I wrote back:

"When do you know if it's you or me
When does a dream ever seem
Like in the middle of the night
It's really daylight
and a dream isn't a dream anymore
(and the waves never reach the shore!)
WHO IS TO SAY WHAT'S FALSE OR TRUE
IS IT ME? OR IS IT YOU?
But hiding behind what's true or false
is not the only thing lost
It's feeling
deep inside
of a love, it only tried!"

He wrote back that he hoped I realized just how much I had going for me, either with or without him. He told me that he knew that if I followed my instincts, there would be no mountain I could not climb, no sea I could not swim in, or no sky I could not fly in.

I interpreted it as a trivialization of what I meant to him. How could he even mention anything about "with or without me in your life" when we had become so close to one another? I wrote:

"Billy Ray,
I'll always be your FRIEND, it's
just so damn hard not being more.
My heart, K."

Then he wrote back that he was just glad to have gotten to meet me and to know me. He said that he had so much respect and admiration for me and that he just liked me. He said that my feelings of strength and positiveness were everything he had ever learned and studied, but that he had been knocked down so many times that he was afraid to use them for himself. He asked me if I understood and asked me to circle a "yes" or a "no" he had included in the note.

I understood. The only thing I could not understand was why he was even asking me after all we had already been through - after our times together. Shouldn't our lovemaking at the Martha Washington Inn and our talk over coffee at Shoney's - believing in each other to fulfill each others' dreams - be as fresh on his mind as it was on my own?

My mind screamed at me "Leave now with your self-respect, somewhat jolted, and bask in his admiration of the powerful woman that you know you are. Go back to Nashville and keep working day and night trying to get him signed to a major label even though he is still signed with Scott. Let fate take the reins instead of trying to ride this wild pony yourself."

Instead of listening to my voice of reason, I circled the "yes" and we talked about both believing in his dreams. I told him that if we both believed in the same dream as one and had no doubts, then that dream would surely come true.

Then he kissed me and I lived out all of the dream - being with the man I loved whom I could now visualize at the height of success and happiness. Fate would allow that dream to come true because the man I loved really is where he wanted to be all along. And perhaps I am where he wanted me to be all along.

Chapter 8

My Visit To Billy Ray's Home

I had no sooner gotten in from The Comfort Inn and unpacked my dirty clothes when Billy Ray called to tell me that Cindy, his spouse, was going to be out of town for a few days. Cindy worked for a cigarette advertising company and occasionally had to leave on business. He invited me to visit him at his home. I was anxious to be with Billy Ray and relive some of his childhood escapades with his two best friends, Jimmy and Calvin, that he so often told me about, but I was hesitant and apprehensive at the same time. My mind was bombarded with thoughts. What if Cindy came back while I was there? How would we manage to keep it a secret from their neighbors? Why would he ask me to come be with him there if their house meant anything to him at all?

We had five back-and-forth phone conversations that night before I agreed. I had such strong arguments that even Billy Ray had second thoughts. He told me that his family's cemetery was there and that maybe one day I would want to be buried there, next to him - such a morbid suggestion but one that finally made me rationalize that he really did love me if he could ask me to join him there, in the home he shared with his wife, or in a burial plot he wanted me to see. I knew that if I did go, once I left, my memory would linger long thereafter and he would always be reminded of my having shared his home with him as if we were man and wife.

I arrived in Ironton, Ohio, late the next night. I went to the designated pay phone at the corner market down the road from his house and with shaking hands, finally found a quarter. When he answered the phone, I informed him of my arrival and he quickly hung up. Before I could return my wallet to my purse, he appeared as if he were superhuman, a characteristic I had often suspected. He told me that this was the very pay phone he used at night when he wanted to tell me he loved me. He would tell Cindy he was going out to run and instead would jog to the corner and call me collect.

I followed him to his house and parked in front of their home. When we walked in, the room was illuminated only by the light from the Christmas tree which was beautiful with angels and pink ribbons and presents spilling out onto the floor. It was somewhat reminiscent of the beautiful tree at the Martha Washington Inn. This tree, however, did not give me the same, warm, inviting feeling when I looked at it. Instead, I felt cold and empty. I told Billy Ray how uncomfortable I felt about being there. After all, I was dressed in bright blue cowboy boots and a neon yellow jacket over jeans. I told him there was no way the neighbors could not have spotted this Porter Waggoner look alike. He paid no heed to this and told me to sit down for a minute while he moved my car to the shed behind his house.

I sat down mechanically and stared numbly at the mantle full of smiling pictures of Billy Ray and Cindy. Billy Ray's cat, Mr. Sly, slinked around my ankles as if checking me out and making sure I was acceptable. I passed his test. Little did I know that this cat would be forever immortalized in Billy Ray's 1993 hit, "Where'm I Gonna Live When I Get Home?".

Billy Ray reappeared in the kitchen door and asked if I was hungry. I suppose I answered affirmatively because he came back with ham and cheese sandwiches on hamburger buns and potato chips.

After snacks and several beers, Billy Ray asked me to call the studio where he had recorded "The Babysitter" to see if we could arrange to re-cut the vocal track while I was in town. He was dissatisfied with the song and somehow viewed my visit as an opportunity to re-record it. My pre-phone call pep talk was simply Billy Ray asking, "You will do anything for me, won't you?" Ignoring his overt manipulation, I called the studio and arranged to re-mix and put on new vocals the next day.

Billy Ray was happy with this, so I attempted to clear my mind from thinking that my visit had been calculated all along.

We then popped some popcorn and drank a few more beers. After laughter and love-talk, Billy Ray decided he wanted to show me his pet raccoon at his Mom's house, the home where he had grown up. We turned out the lights on his pickup before we got to the driveway and pretended we were raccoon burglars as we sneaked into the backyard. He pointed to a cage. Upon gazing inside, I saw the biggest, fattest raccoon I had ever seen in my life. It seemed more like a small bear.

Billy Ray gave me a brief tour of the place and told me more funny stories about his childhood.   I became so caught up in his antics and story-telling that I forgot all about how uneasy I was before.

Here I was with the man I loved, the man with whom I thought I would spend the rest of my life, in a house where he lived with the woman who shared his name.

Billy Ray must have sensed my feelings, because he came to me, held my face in his hands and kissed me tenderly - one of those kisses that left me so weak I thought I would have to hold on to something to keep from falling. I already had fallen and Billy Ray assured me that he had, too. Later that night, I pushed aside any feeling of guilt or nervousness that I felt and gave myself to Billy Ray. We slept closely that night in their king-size bed.

The next morning, we ate cold popcorn for breakfast and

washed it down with Alka Seltzer Cold Plus and generic aspirin.

We then began our journey that day to the hills of West Virginia, where Billy Ray's friend Paul Moore operated his studio in a double-wide trailer. We arrived at the studio where we drank warm coffee and cold beer and re-mixed "The Babysitter." This studio was a far cry from the sophisticated, Music Row studios to which I was accustomed.

Later that day, as we rode around the countryside, Billy Ray showed me more of the sights of his hometown. I even got a glimpse of the Auger Inn, a honky-tonk that inspired him to write a song called "Auger Inn, Stagger Out." The man can write a song - probably because his life *is* a country song, lacking only resolve to bridge the verses.

When we returned to the house, he gave me a pair of yellow sweat pants and a Gold's Gym t-shirt. We were starving and decided to order pizza. The phone rang and he sprinted upstairs to the bedroom to answer it because he knew it would be Cindy. Just as I was answering the door for the pizza, I heard him say, "I love you, too." Those same words which so often raised my heart into the heavens now pierced my soul.

Even though I was famished before we ordered the pizza, my appetite was somewhat diminished by what I had just overheard, but I decided not to mention it to Billy Ray.

We read to each other for a while from the book *Cybernetics*, a gift I had given him, blatantly displayed on the coffee table complete with an inscription from me to him. We decided to call it an early night since I had to leave at five in the morning in order to catch a plane for a show in Toronto, Canada.

Billy Ray spent an awfully long time that night in the bathroom with the water running before coming to bed. I later learned that he was throwing up because of having consumed to excess. We laid in each other's arms and I held him tightly as he slept while I stared at the ceiling.

At 3:30, my confused state still had not allowed me to drift off to sleep. My mind raced with the thoughts I so desperately tried to push out of my head. I climbed out of bed and dressed in the dark. He awakened and immediately asked me what was wrong. I lied that I couldn't fall asleep because I was thinking about the trip home and making my plane. He told me to finish getting dressed while he made some coffee. I drank a cup while he drew me a map showing me how to get back to the interstate. He also made me promise faithfully that I would not read a note he had written upon the back of the map until I had arrived safely home.

Six and a half painfully long hours later - not painful from driving, but painful because of our separation - I stood in my kitchen and read the other side of the map he had drawn. It read:

"I love you 4 ever
Nothing can ever change that.
I'm glad we shared our time together
It was beautiful (except for when I got sick). . ."

I trembled as I clung to that piece of paper as tightly as I had clung to Billy Ray the night before. I would have never dreamed it possible taking into account all of the nervousness and indecision I felt before I left, but I loved this man even more than ever, even if he had a weak stomach.

Chapter 9

The Ragtime Lounge

As Billy Ray's contract with Scott Faragher neared its completion, he began to spend more and more of his time at Del Reeves Productions. He did nothing short of beg us to begin our campaign to promote his career. I knew Dad was hesitant to make plans to go into the studio with him since he had not yet signed a contract with us. Signing a contract hinged upon Dad's approval of Billy Ray as a performer. Dad had not seen Billy Ray perform and his schedule, however unfortunately, had not allowed him time to go all the way to the Ragtime in West Virginia to see Billy Ray live. By now, I had seen Billy Ray perform on many occasions - both on and off stage - and I sung praises of his entertaining to Dad. I conveniently omitted his off stage abilities since I saw no need for Dad to know of our involvement because I knew it would kill the deal and Dad would probably kill me. . . or Billy Ray.

On December 15, 1988, Billy Ray mailed me a cartoon he had drawn depicting his freedom from Scott. I knew he was happy about this because the drawing contained several clown faces. I had talked to him just before he received the release papers and he had told me how he thought he would have a t-shirt made that read "Punch Me" because that was what he felt happened on his weekly visits to Nashville.

I finally managed to find a break in Dad's schedule around the 21st of December so I penciled Billy Ray into the books. Billy Ray was anxious to get Dad to go into the studio with him and was insistent on using his own musicians. I knew from past experience that Dad would want to use the A-Team musicians out of Nashville. The A-Team is a group of session players who play on almost all of the hit records which are recorded in the city.

In order to divert a disagreement between Billy Ray and Dad, I kept Dad busy in the studio producing and mixing every day before our trip. On the day we planned to leave, I drove out to the house to meet Mom and Dad. Dad had mustered up a little enthusiasm over the trip and offered to start out driving and let me take over after a little while. He, however, was still "Looking at the World Through A Windshield," as his song implied, when the three of us pulled into the Ramada Inn outside of Huntington, West Virginia. We checked in, grabbed a bite to eat, and went to our room to prepare for our big night at the Ragtime Lounge.

We had considerable difficulty locating the lounge because Dad kept insisting that we must be on the wrong side of town. The area was dark and ominous. The few buildings that remained standing were gloomy and intimidating.

Finally, the neon glow of a honky tonk came into sight. Billy Ray himself came outside to escort us into the dark and smoky bar. Dad turned to me and yelled over the noise, "We'll be lucky to make it out of here alive!" Just then, people started shaking our hands and offering to buy us drinks and asking Dad to "Doodle-do-do-do" for them. "Doodle-do-do-do," Dad's famous trademark, is a part of his song "Girl on the Billboard." When he was preparing to record the song, Johnny Cash told him that he needed something to make it distinctive. It was then that Dad adopted his trademark after Johnny's suggestion.

We were seated at a table in center stage as we anticipated experiencing the full impact of the Cyrus hurricane. Billy Ray was dynamic and the crowd was crazed. They knew every word to every song and sang along with him. Dad commented that he thought women would have thrown themselves from the balcony if the place had only had a balcony. Billy Ray even asked Dad to join him onstage to sing "Girl on the Billboard" and "Dime at a Time" with him.

We decided to leave after the second set. Billy Ray asked Dad for permission to stop by on his way home so that he could talk to me - we would just sit outside on the hotel's swing. Dad consented and I felt doubly relieved because he had been so impressed by the performance and also because he did not suspect my involvement with Billy Ray.

I waited for him in the hotel lobby. It wasn't long before a figure in a long, black coat and fingerless gloves opened the door. I thought the little lady behind the desk would faint - was it her dream or mine that had just appeared from the moonlit night? Billy Ray asked if I wanted to swing or go on a sightseeing tour. I opted for the pre-dawn tour.

Billy Ray drove up to a hill overlooking the Ohio River. On one side of the river was Ohio and on the other side was West Virginia. We climbed out of his truck and into the cold night. It was a beautiful, crisp, cold night and the lights danced delicately upon the water. He pointed to the direction of his house and asked me if I wanted to spend the night with him and Cindy. I adamantly declined. He then admitted that he had hoped I would turn down the offer but that he nevertheless felt obligated to ask me.

We drove back to the hotel and pulled into the deserted parking lot where the light of morning was barely gracing the edge of the sky. We decided to say goodnight before it was time to say good morning, but not before our primal instincts towards one another culminated in a fast and furious fashion in the front seat of his little red pick-up truck.

It seemed as if I had just returned to the room and closed my eyes when I heard a knock at the door. I jumped up and tried not to disturb Mom and Dad. I opened the door and saw Billy Ray smiling at me.

I smiled back at him, fully aware that I must have looked a mess. I told him to wait and closed the door to the room. I threw on some clothes and woke Mom and Dad. I dressed quickly and told Dad that Billy Ray and I would go down and pick up some coffee for them. If I had learned anything during my ten years on the road with Dad, it was just how crucial that first cup of coffee in the morning is. It is virtually impossible to converse with him in the morning until he has had his coffee complete with two creams and three sugars!

Billy Ray and I went downstairs, after waiting forever on the elevator, picked up the coffee, delivered it to Dad and told him that we would wait in the restaurant for them while we each had our much-needed caffeine.

Billy Ray and I finally boarded the elevator, after passing time in the hall with kisses, and as I was about to push the down button, I turned to him with a sparkle in my eye and asked him if he wanted to go up or if he would like for me to go down. He answered my question when he pulled the emergency stop in the elevator and gave me the best wake-up call I had ever received.

We were sitting at the table and the waitress had just delivered our cups of coffee when Mom and Dad walked in. Dad immediately grumbled, "We could've been here sooner but we had to wait on the damn elevator."

Billy Ray and I glanced guiltily at each other but quickly averted our eyes. I felt color rising onto my cheeks as I desperately tried to avoid making eye contact with Billy Ray because I knew I would burst into a fit of hilarious laughter.

———————

Chapter 10

Our First Christmas

Christmas was fast approaching and I had no idea what to get Billy Ray for a Christmas present. I wondered if I should even get him anything at all. We hadn't broached the subject. I wanted desperately to get him something special - something that showed him how much I cared for him, but I knew that no matter what I got him, he wouldn't be able to take it home.

As difficult as it was to do holiday shopping under normal circumstances, it was even more difficult to shop for a man who was somebody else's husband. I decided to go looking anyway and I found myself at one of my favorite New Age bookstores.

I finally found the perfect gift for Billy Ray: a miniature castle. I made a homemade card where I wrote:

"Billy Ray,
To the king of my heart,
king of my dreams
and king of my castle.
I love you,
Kari."

To my utter astonishment, Billy Ray gave me his sacred, *TNT—Power Within You* book. He inscribed on the inside:

"Kari,
My wonderful, beautiful friend. . .Only you can understand
me, the way I think, the way I feel, what makes my heart beat
and my world go round. Therefore, I trust that only you
could possibly understand my gift and how much it means to

me and for me to want you to have it. This is my Bible as you may recall me telling you about it that magical night in room 115 when we read its scriptures. You may also recall me telling you about the old man Chiropractor, Dr. Bailey, in Flatwoods who gave this book to me, and more than this book, he gave me his love and belief in myself and in my dreams. . ."

The castle remains with me still. Every Christmas Eve since then, I pull out that book - what Billy Ray said was a worn, frayed, torn, used and abused part of him. Now I don't laugh, but I reflect on all our blessings and all of life's challenges we have conquered. Now I can only wish him love and peace within himself and hope that his dreams will always continue to come true.

———————

Chapter 11

New Year, New Contract

The New Year brought with it an increased determination in my efforts to elevate Billy Ray to star status. I had selflessly adopted this goal as my one New Year's Resolution.

Shortly after our trip to the Ragtime, I did not have too hard a time convincing Dad that Billy Ray was worthy of our attentions. Soon thereafter, Billy Ray readily agreed to sign a contract with Del Reeves Productions. Billy Ray insisted that he call his dad before he signed the contract. His dad, Ron Cyrus, spoke to my father and was excited that his son was finally going to get somewhere. He told Dad that he had seen him on television and sensed that he was an honest man. He also said that he was involved in politics in Kentucky and knew how to distinguish between people he could and could not trust. With his father's blessing, Billy Ray thus signed our contract. The contract, known as a Production Agreement, entitled Del Reeves Productions, Inc., to eight percent of the suggested retail price of all records sold from his first album with a major recording label, providing the major record deal, and fifteen percent of his gross earnings for the term of such a contract. We, in turn, would fulfill the roles of manager, and producer. My Mom signed the Investor Agreement, in which she assumed the role of financing a part of Billy Ray's career. Although we were pitching four other acts at the time, I devoted every possible second to Billy Ray's cause.

Billy Ray convinced me that our being together somehow hinged upon his attaining his dreams of stardom. He told me that he hoped I understood that if he didn't make it as a star, he would still be living in Ironton, Ohio, but his heart would always be with me. At times like that, he would make me feel as though I were a fringe benefit that was included in the contract he had recently signed with us. Although I was aware of his tactics, I nonetheless devoted more and more of my time to him and to his career.

My apartment became a hotel of sorts whenever Billy Ray was in town. I even dubbed it "Hotel Belmont," due to its close proximity to Belmont University. It was cheaper for the company than paying his tab at the Shoney's Inn or the Hall of Fame Hotel, an unnecessary expense since his nights would be spent with me anyway. It did not prove much of a bargain for me, since, in the end, the price was my heart.

Before we left the office at night, Billy Ray always called Cindy. I would leave the room but my bad timing usually forced me to hear him end their conversation by telling her that he loved her too.

Every time he hung up the phone, he would look at me and say that he was a misunderstood man whom only I could understand. He seemed genuinely sorry that I had to hear his profession of love.

I never imagined not waking up to Billy Ray, even when I knew he was at home waking up to his wife. My mind simply pretended that he was on the road entertaining millions of adoring fans. I convinced myself that I should feel happy rather than lonely. It would be much later that I learned even when he awoke on the road, at times he was not alone, nor was he with his wife.

When we did greet the day together, especially on Wednesday mornings, I knew he was getting ready to pack up that little red truck and head back to his other life in Ironton, Ohio. Instead of dwelling on this, our daily regimen would begin with me starting coffee and plugging in a subliminal message on the stereo for him - either positive thinking tapes or some of our favorite songs that had meaning.

Then I would make us a "stamina breakfast drink" - not that Billy Ray required a breakfast drink to keep up his stamina - consisting of a banana and milk and an energy source called Vital 18 that I would buy at the health food store.

During our mornings together, I got Billy Ray hooked on the music of Frankie Miller. The song "I'd Gladly Go Blind (If I Could See You One More Time)" became our own special theme song. This eventually prompted me to slightly alter the lyrics to "I'd Gladly Go Blind (If I Don't Get You Signed)."

It was one of those Wednesday mornings when Billy Ray was preparing to leave - going back unsigned and feeling low. I made coffee and flipped on Frankie - a smoking rendition of "Do It 'Til We Drop" which should cure any blues. Billy Ray had gathered his belongings, and stuffed his grubbies, tapes, and my heart into a duffel bag, and walked out my backdoor. Just as he was ready to turn the key to unlock the door to his little, red GMC truck, the song "I'd Gladly Go Blind" came on and he looked up at me like a hungry, lost cat and ran up the stairs to my apartment. Without a word, he pushed me up against the sink and kissed me hard and then harder. I threw him on the linoleum, pulled down his black sweat pants and opened my robe. I completed my morning aerobics class without ever having to leave for the gym.

Despite these precious mornings when we awoke lying side by side, thoughts of his other life took hold of me all of the time. In order to ward off the thoughts that crept into my head, I devoted my entire self to Billy Ray's career. The quest for a recording deal was gaining little headway so Billy Ray suggested I find him a writers' deal. I shifted gears and started dialing publishing companies. My efforts were frequently met with statements about how the publishers already had too many writers. The astronomical number of songs we received at the office daily attested to the validity of this, but I remained committed to Billy Ray's cause and continued in my efforts.

I succeeded in getting Billy Ray appointments with Tree Publishing and Opryland Music Group, two international giants in the publishing world. Both companies were extremely helpful and eventually pitched us some great material that Billy Ray and the Players played in their live performances. The deal I sought remained elusive, but I felt good that I could at least introduce Billy Ray to some influential people in the music business.

I take small comfort now in realizing that my hard work paid off for Billy Ray in terms of his career. I never entertained the idea that I would not be by his side when his time came.

———————

Chapter 12

Capitol Rejection

After his Sunday night performances at the Ragtime, Billy Ray made bootless attempts to come to my apartment. Although he assured me that he wanted to be with me all the time, often his words and actions did not match. He seemed more interested in having a record released than having his boots removed and only came when business called.

Regardless, those Monday mornings when we awoke in each other's arms always got my week off to a good start. On this particular morning, I excitedly prepared for a meeting with Capitol Records, which I had arranged on behalf of Billy Ray.

He smiled at me through droopy eyelids as he gave me a pep talk for the meeting. He reassured me that there was nothing as powerful as an idea whose time had come, a favorite quote he had borrowed from Victor Hugo and his *TNT* book. We both believed that the time had come for the world to hear his music. However, convincing the record companies to believe it was proving to be a major obstacle. What the world wants to hear and what record companies want the world to hear are two separate animals altogether.

My biggest decision of that morning was choosing what to wear - the right "power" dress for the meeting. As I stood in front of my closet in my bra and pantyhose, I glanced over at that gorgeous, naked man beneath my sheets who was watching me intently. I decided to postpone the decision and took off what little I had on. I decided that I had more pressing business to tend to - giving Billy Ray a proper wake-up call.

Afterwards, Billy Ray promised me that he would come down to see me every week whether or not he had any music business. He reminded me that he loved me and that our love was the only thing that mattered to him.

This alone enhanced the urgency of my situation and I left for the meeting more determined than ever to make Billy Ray a star.

I met with Terry Choate and watched anxiously as he kept time to Billy Ray's music with a set of drumsticks which he tapped rhythmically on the conference table. Although I interpreted this as a good sign, when I walked out of his office my ears rang with the advice I had been given: that Billy Ray's music was lacking in direction.

On the brief ride back to my apartment, I cleared my head of the negative thoughts bombarding my brain and decided that I would not let Billy Ray know how discouraged I was.

I returned to the apartment to find Billy Ray still in bed, so he literally took the news lying down. I told him not to let this piece of advice phase him. I assured him that we would show Capitol direction with the new, original songs we planned to record at Allisongs.

I spent the next day trying to arrange meetings in an effort to convince someone - *anyone* - else that Billy Ray's time had come. I was disgusted by the indecision exhibited by the record labels to which my Dad and I had pitched Billy Ray's material. It was difficult to imagine then, when at times our plight appeared hopeless, that Billy Ray, a mere two years later, would be on top of the music world.

———————

Chapter 13

Demo Sessions

I rarely had an occasion to talk to Cindy at length because Billy Ray would try to call me when she wasn't at home or have me call him at the gym in Ashland, Kentucky, or he would jog to the infamous pay phone on the corner and call me collect.

One night he phoned me before going home after another night of captivity at The Ragtime and said that he and Cindy had listened as I left a message on their answering machine that afternoon as they lay in bed. Although he said that they were laughing about the overly-exuberant message I had left, it was disheartening to think of the two of them paired together in bed. It was even more painful to think about them laughing at me.

The longest conversation I ever had with Cindy was the night she called the office to inquire about Billy Ray's arrival. Billy Ray and Terry were driving in for a demo session the following day. I told her that they had not yet appeared and that I was uncertain as to whether they were going to the office first or going straight to the hotel. She asked me to have Billy Ray call her as soon as possible and explained that her grandfather had passed away. I expressed my sincere sympathies and I promised that I would go to the hotel to wait on them if they didn't show up at the office soon.

When Terry and Billy Ray walked in the front door, I was sitting in the lobby of the hotel. Billy Ray said he was pleasantly surprised to see me, but I explained that the news I had was not very pleasant and I told him what had happened. He excused himself and left to use the pay phone in the hallway while Terry and I adjourned to the lounge. Billy Ray joined us there shortly. I offered to reschedule the session for him in case he wanted to go back home to Cindy. He said he had made arrangements with Cindy to stay in Nashville that night and leave immediately following the session tomorrow.

The guys were starving, so I took them to Longhorn Steaks and bought them dinner. On the way back to the hotel, we stopped and bought a six-pack of beer.

Back at the hotel, Billy Ray and I sat on one bed and Terry sat on the other while we discussed the session. Terry seemed a little apprehensive because of his lack of experience in the studio, but Billy Ray and I convinced him that he would do a fabulous job.

I went to the bathroom and when I walked out, Billy Ray had the phone in his hand and said he was calling home. I excused myself by telling him that I was going down to the lobby for something. A few minutes later, he came down looking for me and asked me why I had left.

I told him, "It's pretty simple. I think you would be able to figure it out. You were calling home and I didn't want to hear the conversation."

He told me he was calling home to talk to his mom and he wanted me to talk to her, too. He promised me that he would have never put me in that position had he been calling Cindy.

I went back upstairs with him and found Terry fast asleep. I climbed into bed with Billy Ray and we kissed and wrestled beneath the sheets. We became so consumed in each other that we forgot all about the person sleeping in the bed next to us.

I woke up early the next morning and did not wake Billy Ray before I went home to shower and change. I had a lot to do before the session - pick up the half-inch tapes, run off copies of the song charts for the musicians, get blank cassette tapes and labels and meet with the engineer, Danny Chauvin, at the studio. As I was ready to walk out my back door after double-checking that everything was turned off, the phone rang and it was Billy Ray. He wanted to ensure that everything was all right. He was concerned since I didn't say anything to him before I had left that morning. I explained that I had a lot to do and I wanted him to be rested and ready to record. I told him I would see him at the studio but first read him an inspirational quote for the day ahead.

The session went unbelievably well. As Billy Ray and I had predicted, Terry did a great job. The guys jammed on "Snooze Ya Lose" and honky-tonked on "Whiskey, Wine, and Beer" and made beautifully sad music on "Suddenly." Billy Ray's vocals were finished and we had just started on Terry's guitar overdubs when we decided to take a lunch break. After a quick fast food feast, Billy Ray asked if he could take a nap at my apartment while we were finishing up at the studio. Terry and I left him there and returned to the studio.

Later, as we drove to get Billy Ray, I thought about how wonderful it felt to be turning the key to the world that I called home - a world in which Billy Ray felt so comfortable that he could be there, too, with or without me.

I drove them back to the studio to pick up Billy Ray's car and ran in to grab a copy of the session. Terry asked that we dub him a copy and we went over to my office where I made extra copies for them. Shortly after they had left, Billy Ray pretended he had forgotten something and reappeared at my door where he hugged me, thanked me, and told me how much he loved me.

As I watched him drive away, I thought about the saying "Death brings people closer together." I thought about how close it brought us the night before - so close, in fact, that it didn't matter that someone was sleeping in the bed next to us.

I tried not to wonder how close it would bring him to Cindy, especially since she was the one who was feeling the pain.

————————

Chapter 14

More Dead Ends

Throughout February and March, Dad and I devoted virtually all of our time to our attempt to make Billy Ray a star. These months became a veritable whirlwind of phone calls, meetings, and, all too often, disappointments.

Dad and I undertook the task of exposing Billy Ray to influential people all over the Music City. We called countless record companies, booking agents, and management companies in an attempt to move Billy Ray one step closer to his dreams of success.

Often, a simple task such as scheduling a single appointment would take weeks. We played numerous games of "phone tag" with representatives from the record companies. We were met with indecision and disinterest so often that, at times, we became exasperated. Yet we persevered and carried the Billy Ray banner into battle.

By the end of February, we appeared to be making some headway in our quest. We had scheduled meetings with three major record labels: Polygam, Capitol, and CBS. In addition, we had an appointment with Jack McFadden, owner of a personal management company. Jack, in our opinion, was *the* personal manager for Billy Ray to have. Currently, he managed the careers of Lorrie Morgan and Keith Whitley. He also served as my father's personal manager back in their California Days in the fifties and sixties, and had managed Buck Owens, as well. Jack would be responsible for advising Billy Ray on every aspect of his career. Dad and I both knew that we needed to get Billy Ray signed quickly. We knew that with Jack's help, there would be no stopping Billy Ray.

We had been trying valiantly to meet with Jack for some time and were excited about the potential of this particular meeting. Despite our high expectations, Jack told us during the meeting that he did not have time to hear Billy Ray's recordings now.

After the meeting, Dad, Billy Ray, and I sat in our office and reflected on what had just happened. Dad was discouraged, as we all were, but he never gave up. Billy Ray told me to write down what had happened and to remind him of it one year from today. Billy Ray told us that he would always remember that day, February 28, 1989, as the day he was scarred for life. He dubbed this "It Ain't Fair" day. We all laughed at Billy Ray's ability to make light of the situation and vowed to continue the battle. None of us considered just how much could transpire in one year.

The next day, I called Jack to see if he had listened to Billy Ray's tapes, but he replied that he had not had time. I tried to rush him by suggesting that we meet again the following week.

The process of bringing stardom to Billy Ray was turning out to be a laboriously long and slow task for all involved. I never promised Billy Ray instantaneous success, but I was honestly surprised that things were dragging on as they were. Dad and I both were doing everything in our power to help him. At times it seemed like we were making no progress, but, in truth, we were making *slow* progress.

As if trying to get Billy Ray a recording contract were not a big enough challenge, we were soon confronted with an even larger battle to fight: the battle with Billy Ray's impatience.

———————

Chapter 15

Frustration

Billy Ray loved this quote: "We get out of life exactly what we put into it, no more, no less. When we put in good thoughts, constructive efforts, and do good, then we receive in return."

It was hard for him to keep positive thoughts first and foremost in his mind. Each morning we awoke in each other's arms in a place where we shouldn't be but wanted to be and in a town where he was wanted, but no one knew it.

I never thought that I was in the wrong place at the wrong time with the wrong person because I was living in a fantasy world. In my mind, we were awakening, not in my one bedroom apartment, but we were rising to the sounds of a city that he loved - a city in which we could open the window and hear car stereos blaring his latest hit, a city where our goals were already achieved. As I walked towards the kitchen to make us coffee, my mind was filled with glittering images of us at the CMA Awards Show and the BMI parties. I could almost hear the thunderous applause as he accepted his Male Vocalist of the Year award.

In reality, I was waking up next to a married man who was miserable in his struggle for success. He could have easily made me equally unhappy if I had let him. But, I refused; I could not let my spirits wane. There were times, however, when I wanted to scream at him.

I had always been told that if you believe the situation you are in is hopeless, then it really is. I believe that if something negative happens, you must take the time to discover that there is a message with a positive lesson in it. If it goes undiscovered, you go about making the same mistakes and inviting more negativeness to cloud your vision.

Billy Ray certainly believed in putting a great deal into life, but he was also a great taker. Like so many other entertainers, his fragile ego often needed to be stroked. Like a baby, he needed to be spoon-fed with compliments and reassurances of his greatness or he would balk. He could be so full of positive energy and enthusiasm when he left, then suddenly sink to the depths of despair. He would then return to singing at The Ragtime, all of his positiveness completely lost. He became impatient. He ranted and raved against Nashville, against me, and against my father. That wonderful, caring, man I had met turned into an overbearing ogre. I tried to calm him by insisting that we were doing all that we could, and that these things took time. I reminded him that loyalty was one of the most important traits to have, especially in this town. We had this conversation on several occasions, but unfortunately, Billy Ray did not take my advice seriously. He had his own agenda.

On Monday, March 13, 1989, Billy Ray called to inform me - the woman who comprised half of his management team, was his co-producer, and who had recently confirmed more meetings with CBS Records and Capitol Records and just talked to Jack McFadden about him - that *he* had arranged meetings with another management firm and with RCA Records on his own.

I was absolutely livid. I told him angrily that trying to represent himself when he already had representation was ridiculous. Unable to think of any other way to express my unhappiness over his actions, I hung up on him.

I quickly dialed Dad's number. He was equally dismayed over Billy Ray's lack of confidence in us. I was angry about his cut-throat tactics and his lack of faith in what we were doing for him. Billy Ray had really thrown us a curve. I could not help but wonder if baseball really *was* his calling!

As soon as I got off the phone with Dad, Billy Ray called back. I screamed and pleaded with him not to go through with the other meeting because I had a meeting scheduled with Jack the next morning. I even offered to call and cancel it for him. I finally convinced him how detrimental this could be to his reputation and for once, he took my advice and conceded to call and cancel the management meeting and I went with him to RCA Records.

I will always remember that instant as the time when Billy Ray gave in and acknowledged that perhaps I did know what was best for his career. This acknowledgment convinced me that Billy Ray *trusted* me.

Chapter 16

The Sacred Candle

Billy Ray and I certainly did share a lot of good times in my funky, Belmont Boulevard apartment. I had little furniture, but lots of love.

Billy Ray and I were dreamers. We imagined we were ship-wrecked on a deserted island, happy to be lost from the cruel music world. Once, when we found an old three-legged table in the attic, it was like finding a true treasure, and, therefore, deserved a ceremony of great rejoice. We lovingly dusted it, adorned it with an empty beer bottle, filed off the end of a peach-colored candle and stuck it in the top. It was our message in a bottle - a message to ourselves that we would never forget our love and commitment to each other.

Before we could light the sacred candle, we had to find a perfect place for the table. Since my living room was sparsely furnished and contained only the essentials - a stereo, television, big pillows, lots of Neil Simon plays, and a plethora of positive thinking books - it was not difficult to find a perfect spot. The focal point of the room, a beautiful picture of Marilyn Monroe lounging languidly under soft, white sheets, was quickly agreed upon as the right place. We placed the table under the photograph in homage to Marilyn. Billy Ray felt the need to further escalate our tribute and insisted that the photograph of Marilyn be kissed each time the candle was to be lit.

We then undertook the task of making up sets of rules to go along with the ceremonial lighting of the candle. I gave Billy Ray a legal pad while I began jotting down my own notes. I wrote what would become Rule #10:

"The keeper of the candle (Party A) is hereby duly acknowledged to use her discretion of when to light the candle when Party B is out of town. This is to uphold the bond that has been waxed by both parties alive. It is to be used when one party is needing the other party through spirit, and soul, or light, through despair, anguish, anger, depression, longing, or just to send the thought that the other party cares. She may strike the match that brings warmth and a laugh to Party B that is miles away, but Party B understands that there is no distance between their love. Two bodies in life may be separated by miles but we always have the love, guidance, and inner strength of each other that time, space, and other humans cannot take away. Therefore, the candles of our souls are always lit to each other."

Billy Ray agreed that this was the perfect summary of the reason for the candle. Anxiously awaiting to hear what he had contributed to our list of rules, I urged him to read me what he had written.

Billy Ray's Rule #3 threw me for a loop. It stated that the table would have to be taken seriously. He had added that if another party should happen to be introduced to the table, then they must love it and believe in it as much as we do.

Stunned, I sat in silence. Then, I grabbed his pen and tried to mark out the words he had written, wishing in vain that I had never heard them.

How could we create a ritual that signified the love between two people and even fathom that another party could ever be introduced to it? How could our ceremony, which stood on sacred ground, engulfed in sacred surroundings, and was to become not only a centerpiece in my living room, but in my lonely nights without him, be turned into something that obviously meant nothing to him?

I suppose bells should have sounded in my head, or perhaps the Liberty Bell should have come crashing down on my thick skull, but my love for Billy Ray prompted me to ignore his rule.

After hours of having lit the first candle and watching it burn brightly, he came to me and kissed me. He told me that Marilyn was watching us. He stood before me and slowly took my clothes off. I laid across the pillows on my floor as he knelt down and wrapped his arms around me to cushion me. That night, we shared something even more sacred than our sacred candle.

The candle was my lighthouse when Billy Ray and I were apart. The flame burned so brightly not just on the candle, but in our hearts - it was a flame I thought would never die.

Chapter 17

Leaving the City

While things in regards to Billy Ray's career were not moving along quite as quickly as we might have liked, I decided to make a move of my own. In early Spring, I vacated my Belmont Boulevard apartment and moved into a farmhouse in Lyles, Tennessee, roughly an hour's drive away from the Nashville city limits. When I packed up my belongings, I packed all the precious memories of the times I had spent there with Billy Ray. My parents were soon to be moving into the larger house on the farm and I welcomed the opportunity to be closer to them.

The first time Billy Ray drove out to the farm with me, he fell in love with the place. We walked in the woods, and around the ponds and fed the catfish and saw a water moccasin. I showed Billy Ray the main house which Mom and Dad would eventually move into. We then threw a softball until darkness fell, then drifted back to my house.

Sometime in the middle of the night as we lay in each others' arms listening to the quiet stillness all around us, I arose to visit the bathroom. As always, I peeked out into the darkness to ensure that the world outside was okay. It was then that I noticed I had left the lights on in the big house. I went back to the bedroom and was quietly searching for my sweats when Billy Ray woke up and asked me what I was doing. I told him I was going to run up to the house and turn the lights off. He insisted that he wanted to go with me but that he did not want to put his clothes on. We ran through the balmy night, hand-in-hand, deliciously naked, and carefree, laughing all the way.

I watched later that evening as Billy Ray stood at the back door gazing at the stars and breathing in the air. I could tell by the way he instantly made himself at home that he loved the place as much as I did.

Billy Ray contributed far more to my little paradise than his mere presence. One day he arrived at the farm with two adorable ducks he had carried in a cardboard box in his back-seat all the way from Greenup County, Kentucky. I had an abundance of snakes, beavers, deer, seasonal Canadian Geese, and well-stocked ponds full of rainbow trout and catfish, but I had no ducks until Billy Ray arrived with the pair that I named Bonnie Wuzzie and Clyde Fuzzie.

We took them out of their paper house and allowed them to waddle into the greens and waters of Lyles, Tennessee. The ducks became our obsession that day. We walked up to the barn in search of loose plywood, hay, strong nails and a hammer, which we collected and used to build them a water-front condominium.

The experience that Billy Ray and I shared that day is one of my most cherished memories of our times together and will be forever etched in my mind. His love of animals matched my own and his contributions did not end with the ducks.

After living on the farm for a while and having numerous talks with Billy Ray about his Mom, Ruth Ann, and how she adored cats, he persuaded me to get a kitten from her. I was hesitant at first, but Billy Ray finally convinced me to give her a call.

I was nervous that night I dialed her number. This was my first chance to make an impression on the mother of the man with whom I intended to spend my life. Naturally, I wanted to make a good impression. I was relieved when she seemed so nice on the phone and volunteered an earful about her son.

A couple of weeks later, Billy Ray brought my little bundle of joy to me. He was gray and white striped with big round eyes. I think he could have easily landed a job in a Friskee's commercial. He really was one adorable kitten. Like Billy Ray, he stole my heart at first glance.

I really don't agree with keeping pets indoors since I think they were born to run in the wild and frolic in nature, but I made an exception for my new kitten. I let him move right into the house with me.

I studied my gift of the tattered *TNT* book diligently in order to come up with a name for my new pet. The chapter on how pipe dreams become realities provided my answer. In the third paragraph, it read: "You would not be a normal, average human being if you did not have hidden desires and so-called pipe dreams. While you may not confess them to anyone, you do build air castles on occasion, seeing yourself doing something or going somewhere or having something—and you take a certain joy just imagining, for the moment, that these air castles are real."

The chapter goes on to say that most people do not give any merit to these feelings because they do not have the faith to follow them through. I had faith that Billy Ray and I would be together forever and I decided to name the kitten Piper, short for "pipe dreams".

Piper served as a source of comfort for me when Billy Ray was away. I could take one look at that kitten and be immediately surrounded by warm thoughts of Billy Ray and all of the things we shared. Piper was just one of the many splendid things that Billy Ray brought into my life.

One night, Piper was no where to be found. I had purposely left all of my windows up in case he came home from chasing mice and wanted in. About two in the morning, I thought I heard an animal cry, so I grabbed my flashlight and looked carefully around the yard, but was unable to find anything.

The next morning my neighbor was out working the ponds behind our houses and said he had found my Piper in one of the spring water runoffs earlier. He didn't want me to see Piper so he had taken care of his burial. Apparently, Piper was on his way home and had fallen into one of the weirs. The cry I had heard, I had heard too late.

I was heartbroken by the loss of Piper, a gift from Billy Ray's mother. However, I reasoned that if the only tragedy I would have to go through was the loss of a few special gifts, I would be lucky. I never imagined that I would have to suffer the loss of the most precious gift of all: the love that I shared with Billy Ray Cyrus.

———————

Chapter 18

Life on the Farm

Either my car was in the shop or I just felt like rednecking on Music Row that day in my Dad's seventy-something, white Silverado pick-up complete with chrome visor, chrome running boards, a souped-up engine, and a chrome quarter horse hood ornament.

After a grueling day of trying to turn Billy Ray's Nashville nightmare into sweet dreams of success, we jumped in the truck and headed out to my house in the holler. It was a fragrant summer evening which followed a hot and humid day that turned into afternoon thunderstorms. We had a bag of Ruffles, two six-packs of Stroh's Lite and Michelob Dry between us as I turned off Highway 100 to cruise the back roads home.

Billy Ray and I were laughing and listening to Shannon's show on KDF when he yelled for me to stop. I slammed on the brakes and he asked if I'd ever put frogs on the hood to see how long they could stay there. I replied quizzically that I, indeed, had heard of frog gigging but never of frog hooding.

Since it was a rainy, Southern, summer night, the backroads were covered with croaking amphibians seeking warmth from the cooling temperatures. On nights like this, frogs are everywhere - perhaps hopping from one lily pad to the next or maybe going out for free flies at the local watering hole. Regardless of the reason, the frogs are all out in ribbiting force. Billy Ray jumped out of the truck, plucked a fresh frog from the road, and plopped it right on the hood of the truck near the windshield.

The entire 9.8 country miles home, we stopped to pick up

frogs and place them upon the hood. I picked up a few myself, but Billy Ray was far more skilled at the trick than I was. I reasoned that it was simply an innate instinct he had that allowed him to handle all of the slimy creatures in the music business.

I jokingly propositioned Billy Ray with the challenge of a rousing game of leap frog once we got back to my house. We laughed hysterically over those frogs and how quickly they flew off the hood of the truck.   Billy Ray's antics never failed to keep me in stitches.

When Billy Ray wasn't cutting up and exposing me to some bizarre form of amusement that I had not yet experienced - like the frogs - he kept me amused with the stories he would tell.   He was constantly quoting people or telling stories that he had heard before. I especially welcomed his original tales. His insecurities never allowed him to believe that he was funny. He saw himself as an unhappy man with troubles that stemmed back to his childhood. He said he always pictured himself as a funny-looking little boy with oversized front teeth and big ears. He was so self-conscious that he said he made friends by trying to be funny to compensate for his looks. It is hard to believe that this gorgeous guy felt he had to compensate for his looks.

Of all of Billy Ray's stories there was one in particular of which I could never tire of hearing. Each time he told it there would be a rush of tenderness in his voice and the excitement he had felt would come back as if it happened only yesterday. That was the story of his mother, Ruth Ann, and the piano.

Ruth Ann didn't have it particularly easy raising her sons on her own. The one thing in which she found comfort was music, especially the piano.

Long before one Christmas, Billy Ray began planning his surprise. He saved his lunch money and hoarded every nickel. Once his funds reached what he thought were suitable proportions, he and his buddies began searching for a piano for Ruth Ann. One day they were out looking and he found an old white upright with a few flowers painted on the front. He knew immediately that this was the present he had to buy for his mother. Barely able to contain his excitement, he and his friends bought the piano, loaded it up, and went back to his house.

He tried desperately to get his Mom out of the house long enough to sneak her present in. He called several more of his friends to get them to assist him with the surprise.

When Ruth Ann drove up in the driveway, she found her yard filled with cars and could hear loud goings-on emanating from within the house.

Billy Ray said that she was not pleased to have walked in on this impromptu "party". She stormed into the house in a furor. Then she saw her darling son standing next to the piano and her anger quickly gave way to tears of joy. Each time Billy Ray told me that story, I could have cried, too. He played on my heartstrings like a true virtuoso.

No one else could ever make me feel the things that Billy Ray made me feel. He would tell me everyday mostly via collect phone calls or in person that he felt the same. He told me that no one could make him smile like I could or make him laugh. He said he had almost forgotten how good it felt to really laugh.

Chapter 19

Play Ball

The warm weather brought with it a heightened awareness of the competitive nature that Billy Ray and I shared. We possessed a mutual love for competition whether it was on the tennis courts, throwing softball, or playing hard ball in bed. Our competitions served as an outlet for our frustrations when the difficulties we encountered in the wacky world of the music industry became too much to bear.

One day, we agreed that a tennis match would do us good. We found the courts at the high school and country club were all in use, so we drove up to Camp Meribah, which was about sixteen miles away from my house. We had one terrific game which I, consequently, won. My victory kiss was not only sweet but salty as we clung to each other, drenched in sweat, hearts pounding, pulses racing in the middle of the court. He yanked my head back and gave me that piercing look of his like he did after one of our love matches.

We rode around the camp and on the makeshift baseball field where the earth was still damp from an earlier summer shower, did donuts in the mud. Billy Ray had just been telling me about his dreams of being a professional baseball player and the excitement he felt as a catcher on an all-star team that had made it to the state tournament.

Afterwards, we both felt so guilty for messing up the infield that we made a promise to buy Camp Meribah a real baseball field when he became famous. As was the case with all of the other promises he had made to me, this one was not kept either.

Later, we drove down the hill to a sign that reads "We're

not mending men but building boys." We then drove into the camp which boasted ponds, a rock quarry and some private trails.

We got out of the truck and climbed in the back to drink beer and absorb the sights of Mother Nature and to enjoy each other. I teased him unmercifully about my victory on the courts. Since I had blown him away on the tennis courts, I blew him away in the back of the pick-up truck, as well. I thought it was only appropriate since I was, as the sign implied, "mending a man" who was unhappy with his marriage and disgusted with the way Nashville was treating him.

————————

Chapter 20

Prayers

Billy Ray and I often talked about religion for hours on end. He once told me that God had talked to him for the first time when he was six years old. He confided that I was the only person in his life that he could talk to about what was in his heart and soul and what he believed in. It upset him that Cindy made fun of his practice in visualization, and thought he was talking nonsense when he suggested that he wanted to go to church. Billy Ray also lamented that Cindy objected to his hanging his list of goals on the refrigerator. This reminded me of the time he had told me that Cindy did not allow him to hang his pictures of Elvis on the wall. Taking into account Billy Ray's devotion to the King, this was a true deprivation.

My own religious upbringing allowed me some insight and understanding of Billy Ray's philosophies. I consider myself a very spiritual person and the ability to share this special part of myself with Billy Ray greatly strengthened our relationship.

I start each day with the Unity Church's "Daily Word" and I say it aloud. I also attend Mass throughout the week. After everyone has left the church, I light candles, kneel on the marble steps, and pray for my family, my friends, for the sick, the needy, for my sins, and then, I would pray for Billy Ray's success and for the day that we could finally be together.

Thus, it was very easy to listen and sometimes help Billy Ray with his own religious queries. I told him that it was not necessary to dress in a Sunday suit and walk into a building to feel holy. I eventually got him hooked on the Daily Word.

He would have me record it for him so that he could listen to the uplifting messages whenever he felt depressed.

Billy Ray and I often bowed our heads and said our prayers aloud together. Once as we drove into Nashville after one of his stays on the farm, we stopped along the roadside because Billy Ray wanted to pick me a bouquet of buttercups. First we walked over to an old oak tree by the bank of the Harpeth River and watched in silence as the water rushed by. Billy Ray broke the silence when he asked if we could pray together, which we did. We then left and hadn't driven very far before Billy Ray remembered that he had forgotten to pick the flowers for me. I told him that it didn't matter because what we shared at the river was more important and would last far longer than the flowers of spring.

Billy Ray used to tell me a story about one of his amazing religious experiences. When he was only twenty-one years old, he and his band Sly Dog were the houseband in a club in Ohio. One night, the club was almost entirely burned in a fire. Billy Ray and his band went by the next day to see if any of their equipment had been spared. Billy Ray found a Bible, untouched by the flames, in the back of a burned amplifier.

Once when he was working out in the gym, Billy Ray ran into an old schoolmate. The friend told him that he was now a minister and invited him to his service. Billy Ray showed up there the next Sunday. He was so excited when he called to tell me about it. The sermon he had heard was about David and Goliath, coincidentally, one of Billy Ray's favorite stories from the Bible. Billy Ray told me he knew it was meant for him to be there on that day. He saved the church newsletter and gave it to me.

I often viewed Billy Ray as David and the music industry as Goliath. I suppose my Dad and I were the slingshot.

———————

Chapter 21

Insensitivity

Despite all of the things we shared, Billy Ray could be extremely insensitive when it came to my feelings. He always said that I was the strongest person he had ever met, so I guess he thought there was nothing I couldn't deal with. But his words often hurt.

The night after his anniversary, he called to tell me all about it, how Cindy was waiting for him to get home from the Ragtime and how she had opened a bottle of champagne and dressed in sexy lingerie. And this was a marriage that was reportedly on the rocks. Warning signs flashed all around me, but I blindly carried on, consumed by my passions to make Billy Ray a star and in turn, spend the rest of my life with him. After all, hadn't he written me an I-love-you-and-nothing-will-ever-change-that note?

Billy Ray's insensitivity also reached a peak during the time he fell off the face of the earth for a week. Perhaps he thought I wouldn't notice he wasn't there to pick up the phone each morning when I called to give him his customary wake-up call. He didn't think I'd miss the collect calls from the gym every afternoon or the calls he made during his breaks at The Ragtime or the two-hour collect calls he made after the show at three in the morning. When he finally got in touch with me, he told me he had been on vacation in Myrtle Beach but that nothing happened between he and Cindy since she had taken a girlfriend along. He didn't feel that it was necessary to call me before he left town for a week. After all, I was only the person with whom he had invested his future both in his business and in his personal affairs. I should have recognized this as an omen of things to come.

I was also the person at whom he directed the wrath of the anger he felt stemming from his not being signed to a record label yet. He never accepted any responsibility for the fact that a record label chose not to offer him a recording contract. Instead, he chose to blame it on me, reasoning that it was something I had done wrong or that I had not dedicated enough time to him.

He never considered that I represented four other independent acts and that I was supposed to be trying desperately to get them signed, as well. Nor did he take into account that I booked my father's dates, responded to tons of mail each day, and answered phone lines which rang constantly. I also ran two publishing companies, pitched songs, and wrote for a magazine. However, none of that mattered. Nothing mattered to him except his selfish desperation to become a star.

I guess I should have figured it out on that night at the Martha Washington Inn when he wrote out his list of goals and included me as the workhorse. I, however, blinded by love, overlooked it then. Now, when I really *was* doing all the work and it was reality - not just writing on a piece of paper - I grew tired of his overbearing tendencies.

Despite the faraway vow he had made to come see me weekly - whether or not he had business to take care of - just because he loved me and wanted to be with me, there were often several week-long spans of time when I did not see him at all. However, when we had an appointment to discuss his career, he showed up. He never missed an opportunity to promote his career, but he never made an opportunity to promote our relationship.

The brunt of his insensitivity came when he told me that he knew that I had given it all up for him, but that if his career did not take off, then he supposed I had given it up for nothing. My hurt and anger finally came to a head as I screamed at him, asking him to put himself in my shoes for once.

His response was a short note saying that he was sorry if he had ever made me feel something less than what I was. He swore on his life that he would never hurt me intentionally. He told me that he wanted to be too, too much to me and that he wanted me to be the same to him. He said he wanted to dream and accomplish those dreams and that he knew that together, nothing could ever beat us. He begged me to be his friend till the day he died and swore he would always be mine.

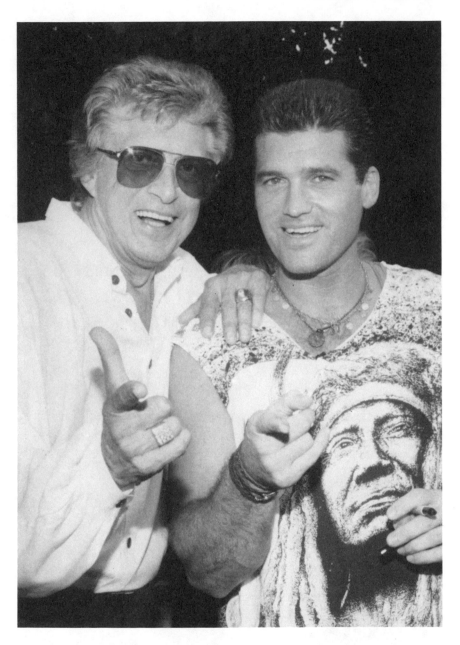

My Dad, Del Reeves, and Billy Ray, during happier days. (Photo by Alan L. Mayor)

Billy Ray and I pose backstage at the Ragtime Lounge in Huntingdon, West Virginia.

Billy Ray, with his Bud Light, and I, with my Stroh's Lite, exhibit our differing beer preferences.

I relax after one of my own performances.

Me, with my hero Roy Acuff, who always made me feel at home backstage at the Grand Ole Opry.

Dad and I pose with our good friend Ed Bruce.

Billy Ray in an early publicity photograph.

Jack McFadden and Dad in a photo taken in 1958 during their California Days.

Dad, Billy Ray, and Merle Kilgore at Billy Ray's Triple Platinum Party at BMI. (Photo by Alan L. Mayor)

Me onstage with my favorite entertainer, my Dad,
Del Reeves.

Dad with the woman in his life, my Mom,
Ellen Reeves.

Dad hams it up with the man he thought would carry
on the Del Reeves Legacy.

The Reeves Girls

Kari Reeves.

Bethany Reeves.

Billy Ray during our trip to the Martha Washington Inn.

Chapter 22

Dull Days, Hot Nights

Having temporarily overcome our disagreements, Billy Ray and I embarked upon a methodical, often mundane routine in our quest for a recording contract. We continued to meet with Jack McFadden but made very little progress. Ironically, as our days became dull and uneventful, our nights became hotter and more impassioned than ever.

Because Billy Ray spent so much time on the farm with me, I began to think of it as our home. Our days were long and grueling and we compensated by making the nights well worth our wait.

One evening, Billy Ray and I reminisced about our night at the Martha Washington Inn. While my bathroom on the farm was not the spacious spa we enjoyed at the Inn, it did not take us long to steam the place up. When we both got into the tiny shower, I banged my head one time too many and we finally gave up and decided to continue elsewhere.

Billy Ray took my hand and led me to bed. He pulled back the sheets and laid me down and dried off my wet body without the benefit of a towel. We became absorbed into each other in a mad, passionate love-thirsty battle, drinking in every moment, every feeling.

Later, I changed the sheets as he sat in my den watching the evening news. He was clad only in a towel, sitting on the floor and eating cold Chinese food. We watched some of *The Tonight Show* before turning off the lights. We laid in bed and talked and he promised me that he never wanted to leave me and I admitted that I never wanted him to. We fell asleep, but later that night I felt him tossing and turning and mumbling about fighting. When I woke him from his nightmare, he explained to me that he could only remember fighting but he was not sure with whom. I told him not to worry because he was only fighting the battle inside himself. He kissed me tenderly and asked how he could love someone so much. I willingly sunk back into the pillows and felt the delivery of his kisses as he took my hands and raised them above my hand as though I were a prisoner. In a sense, I was a prisoner of his love. He held my hands, each finger interlocking and placed his body on top of mine, where we became intertwined as one.

————————

Chapter 23

The Spittoon

I always looked forward to our drive into work. The hour-long ride never lacked in jovial verbal dueling.

We would usually stop by Patton's Park to pick up snacks for our drive into Nashville. He would sometimes order six chicken nuggets, sometimes a dozen, while I made us coffee to go.

One morning as we were paying, he spied a basket of roses next to the cash register and picked out a red rose and gave it to me. He looked at me, asked if I remembered, and kissed me.

Each morning, we would drive past an antique store called The Pack Rat on Highway 100. I have always collected treasures and this was one of my favorite places.

I had recently purchased from there an elaborate gold-framed picture of two lovers locked in a frightful embrace as a wicked-looking old man stood staring at them. The scene reminded me of the spell Billy Ray and I were trying to break so that we could be free to be together, without any wicked conscience hanging over our heads.

Just after we had passed The Pack Rat, Billy Ray asked me to turn my Blazer around because he wanted to go in and find me a treasure. I could not find anything that I thought I could not live without, but he was adamant about finding me something. He fell in love with an odd brass spittoon that cost thirty dollars. I laughingly asked him what I could do with a spittoon. He replied that if he had been turned down by a record label, we could pretend that the spittoon represented the company or person and spit in it.

The store owner and her daughter laughed at us. I convinced Billy Ray that if the spittoon was meant for us to take home then it would still be there the next time we stopped by. I settled, instead, for an old, oil bottle with a rooster on it.

I still have the bottle, but we never went back for the spittoon.

A few days later, we forgot about breakfast at Patton's Park and passed by The Pack Rat without even a second glance. We were depressed because every time we thought we were making progress at a label, we hit a brick wall. What we joked about earlier had now hit home as we realized the despondency of our plight.

Billy Ray went to the office with me while I checked my voice mail before he started on his long and depressing road home.

It was close to noon when I suggested that we grab a burger at McDonald's and sit in the park across the street. After lunch, we walked back to his car to say good-bye. He did not want to leave and asked if we could just go back to the farm for a little while.

Since he could not stay, he followed me there in his car. He could only spend a few more stolen moments with me before he would have to hit the interstate in Dickson and fly to get home in time to do his show at the Ragtime that night.

We held each other as tightly as we could, afraid to let go. When we finally parted, he told me to stay where I was and keep holding onto the dreams. Then he drove away and took my dreams with him.

———————

Chapter 24

Mr. Bones

Throughout the month of May, Billy Ray continued to visit me at the farm as often as possible. As each day became warmer and more glorious than the previous one, Billy Ray and I often had considerable difficulty staying indoors even on Music Row.

I tried to get all of my work done early on Monday afternoons when I knew Billy Ray would be coming into town as to spend as much time on the farm with him as possible.

One afternoon was particularly beautiful and we both wanted to lie in the sun to rid ourselves of our winter pallors. We were both avid sun-worshippers. Billy Ray had even written me a note which began:

"Kari,

You are my sunshine. . ."

We took a comforter outside and spread it out by the pond. I told him I sunbathed in the nude since it was only me and the wild animals out here. I went to the bathroom to get some towels and suntan oil, then joined him on the blanket. He kissed me and I offered to put the oil on for him. Just as I was massaging it into his body, I heard the sound of a truck barreling down the dirt road headed in our direction. I grabbed my t-shirt and threw a towel over Billy Ray just as the UPS man appeared careening his brown mobile up the driveway.

He was definitely smiling as he handed me my package and his notebook to sign for it. I decided to make a delivery of my own when I got back to the blanket.

Our love of outdoor sports also grew as the weather became more pleasant. After an especially grueling day at our office - what I referred to by this point in time as Billy Ray Headquarters - we were ready to leave our troubles on Music Row's door step and pick up some beer at the Jim Dandy market and head home.

On our drive, Billy Ray challenged me to a tennis match - winner choosing the prize of their choice. We put on our athletic armor and headed to the tennis courts behind my old junior high school. After a two hour match, Billy Ray finally beat me and I had to honor whatever bet he saw fit. I wondered if I needed my Dad's pick-up truck for the victory request. He said he wanted something to eat and I had to buy.

He decided he wanted pizza. We ran home, donned our jeans, and trekked the short trip to the town of Dickson to dine at its Pizza Hut. While I was in my closet getting a pair of jeans, he joined me and saw my wide array of hats. He took one of my finely-woven straw hats and placed it on my head. He then held me at arm's length and told me how beautiful I looked. He begged me to wear it and I told him I would only if he wore a hat, as well. We were quite the "hatsome couple" parading into the Pizza Hut. He ordered a medium "Meat Lover's Special," we devoured it, and I picked up the check.

As we were almost home, the song "Do You Believe In Magic?" came on the radio. This spawned a conversation between us about the supernatural. Billy Ray told me how he had always believed in magic and in the supernatural. I was well aware of this fascination of his from previous experience. He often told the story of Mary Magdaline Pitts, a young girl from his hometown who had died in a fire. He insisted that one can still hear her cries of help at the spot where the tragedy had occurred.   He was absolutely intrigued by this bizarre, macabre story.   Because he trusted in my writing - not only to write his life story - but he also wanted to help me write the screen play of the Mary Magdaline Pitts story so we could sell the screenplay to Stephen King.

Billy Ray also described a story about how he was driving home one night and had looked over to see a skeleton sitting in the passenger seat.   He said the skeleton, whom he affectionately dubbed "Mr. Bones," disappeared as soon as he pulled into the driveway.

I wanted to laugh, not out of disbelief, but because of the sheer comic value of the story.   Billy Ray was so serious about the story that I could not, for fear I might hurt his feelings. This was a story he repeated so often that I began to feel like he believed more in Mr. Bones than he did in me.   There were times when I wished I could have vanished, too.   Instead of laughing, I matter-of-factly told him that it did not surprise me because I thought he possessed magical powers.

———————

Chapter 25

Death of Keith Whitley

During that summer, the time I spent with Billy Ray continued to magnify our love.

Before leaving the office on Monday, May 9th, Billy Ray challenged me once again - this time to a one-on-one basketball game. I warned him that he did not know what he was getting himself into. We drove to my farm house and changed and headed towards Centerville, where my parents lived in their home they call Gloryland.

I suggested that we drop by their house and ask Dad if he wanted to play with us. Since he still holds the record at his Sparta, North Carolina, high school for being the highest scorer, I thought he would want to join us in our competition.

I rang the front doorbell and it took some time before he answered. As I told him about the game, I stopped mid-sentence when I realized that he had been crying. I asked him what happened and he told me that he had just been informed that Keith Whitley had died. I started to cry instantly not only for Keith, but for Lorrie Morgan, as well. We had attended the same private school and lived in the same neighborhood in adolescence and had grown up together backstage at the Opry.

I knew Dad would want to be alone with Mom so we said good-bye and Billy Ray and I headed for the barn although I no longer had the heart for shooting hoops. Clouds soon began to fill the sky, hinting that a summer thunderstorm might erupt at any moment. Billy Ray suggested that we just find some quiet place where we could watch the clouds roll by and say some prayers.

I drove to Hickman Springs and went high up on a hill over-looking the Duck River. We prayed as the winds gathered their momentum and the lightning began to strike in the distance. Afterwards, Billy Ray gazed out over the hills and with a determined look in his eyes, told me that he knew right then and there that Jack McFadden would sign him. He told me he would never leave Jack because he would always be there for him and try forever to make up for his loss.

———————

Chapter 26

Billy Ray Signs With Jack McFadden

Billy Ray's prediction regarding Jack McFadden indeed proved true.

Our dealings with Jack McFadden continued throughout the next few months at a slow pace. I could tell that Jack had a genuine interest in Billy Ray, but at times it seemed as if we were barely making any progress.

Before Billy Ray was signed to the McFadden Agency, I became frustrated with the endless succession of meetings that seemed to go nowhere, and decided to take the bull by the horns.

As Dad and I tried desperately to convince Jack to take on Billy Ray and when it seemed we were getting nowhere, I opted for another tactic: I began dropping by Jack's office for little visits.

Jack and I would talk for hours about my family and how lucky Dad was to have such a beautiful wife and daughters and a family that had been together for thirty-seven years. We would also talk about the California days when Jack was my father's manager.

As time wore on, my social calls to Jack increased in their frequency. I nonchalantly hinted about Del Reeves Productions, Inc.'s latest signee, Billy Ray Cyrus, which, of course, was my ulterior motive all along.

When it seemed like we were on the verge of getting the contract we had worked so hard for, I worked even harder for

Billy Ray. As if Billy Ray's impatience were infectious, I finally could withstand no more and tried yet another plan of
attack. I often called and visited Jo McFadden, Jack's wife, to
get the inside scoop on the situation with Billy Ray.

Jo and I had countless conversations about Billy Ray, and
from what I could gather, she, too, had fallen prey to Billy
Ray's charms. She could not say enough about how mature
and impressive he was.

She even called me at the office once to pick my brain for
information about Billy Ray. Of course, he was standing by
my desk when she called. She told me she did not have a bio
or a picture of him and she wanted me to get them for her.

She asked me several more questions about him, including
whether or not he was married. I wrote down the question for
him, waiting anxiously on his response. I was dying to hear
him say that he was getting a divorce. But, he did not.
Instead, he only said that he was married, but it was not a
good situation.

Jo asked me rather bluntly if Billy Ray and I had something going on. Fortunately, before I even had a chance to
answer, she continued by telling me that she was just crazy
about him and she advised me that I should get a hold of him.
Little did she know that he already had.

Since my efforts with Jo were nothing more than an endless succession of probing personal questions, we resumed our
quest with Jack. Dad, Billy Ray, and I continued to meet with
him often - sometimes several times a week.

Finally, on July 24, 1989, Billy Ray, Dad, and I sat in Jack's
office where Billy Ray signed a booking and management contract with McFadden and Associates. I was ecstatic. The good
news for which we had worked so hard and waited so long had
finally come true. However, that was only one of the wonderful things to come.

I had wrongly assumed that Jack had no knowledge of my

relationship with Billy Ray. However, one day when I was visiting the office, he pulled me aside and whispered in my ear that Billy Ray had told him that he loved me.

From that day forward, it became a battle of wits between Jack and me concerning all the reasons that Billy Ray and I should not be together.

During one of my weekly sessions with Jack in which we were having an in-depth discussion about my life, Billy Ray called. Jack answered the phone and told him that he was looking at the most beautiful blonde in the world. When he handed the phone to me, Billy Ray immediately said "Hello, Kari."

Billy Ray informed me that for the first time in our relationship, I was talking to a single man. What I had been waiting to hear for two years was now a reality. I tried to stifle my exuberance since I was looking into the face of Jack.

Although I thought that this was what I had been waiting for all along, little did I know that this was the beginning of the end of my romance with Billy Ray.

Chapter 27

McFadden Takes Over

Billy Ray's impatience soon got the best of him yet again and he became dissatisfied with Jack. If he told me once, it seems he told me five thousand times one of his favorite quotes: "Persistence is to man what carbon is to steel." Dad and I were unfortunate enough to be on the receiving end of his persistence.

Even after Billy Ray was signed with the McFadden Agency, Dad and I continued to play an integral role in establishing his career. Although Jack McFadden was, by contract, Billy Ray's agent, Dad, Mom, and myself were still his friends and he implored us for help with his career. We did our damnedest to get him signed to a major label.

During his first couple of months with McFadden and Associates, he would still call my father and me and beg us to call Jack on his behalf - an attempt to "speed up" the process of making him a star.

Billy Ray even called me once to tell me he was coming into town to meet with a larger management firm because he thought they could do more for him than Jack had been doing. I was completely shocked that he was so readily willing to throw away everything we had labored for in the last few months. I told him that it would be unfair to McFadden and Associates and that there was no way he could have them tear up the contract simply because he was impatient and felt like they were not making his dreams come true quickly enough. Just as I had when he tried to schedule appointments for himself while Dad and I were working valiantly to do the same thing, I offered to cancel the appointment for him.

I became worried about Billy Ray and what would become of him if he did not start trusting his management and having patience where his career was involved. I was afraid that if he was not careful, he would really make a mess of things.

As concerned as I was about his career, I could not help but think about all the other things that remained unresolved. At the time, I did not know where I stood in my relationship with Billy Ray. After all, he was now divorced, but I could not tell that anything had changed between us. In fact, if anything had changed at all, it was that I saw him less often than I ever had. I convinced myself that I was taking things too seriously and expecting too much too soon. I told myself that everything would work out.

* * *

Billy Ray became even more firmly ensconced in Jack's camp. As Jack's training became more rigorous, I saw less and less of Billy Ray.

Jack even sent Billy Ray to media school to teach him what to say in interviews and how to conduct himself with the public. I advised him that no one could tell him who or what or how to be. I told him he could only be himself and that alone would make millions love him and buy his music. In retrospect, I am glad he took my advice, but I only wish that media school had taught him the importance of remembering from where he had come and who had helped get him there.

That situation always reminded me of a story Billy Ray used to tell me that his father had passed on to him. Billy Ray had heard the story so many times that he could repeat it to me verbatim. The story related that most people go through life with blinders on, with only one little station you were born to go through, but if you escaped into a new perspective and see beyond that one spectrum, how you choose to use that knowledge you have learned is entirely up to you - whether you go back to an original station or you keep moving is up to you.

Billy Ray wanted a one-way ticket in the first class star section that would take him across the world but he never wanted to forget where it was he got on and all the exchange stations where he used to get off.

He has that first class ticket now, but has forgotten his promise to wave at all the stations where he used to stop. I'm left standing at the depot with my family, holding onto a suitcase filled only with his dreams.

Chapter 28

The Breakfast

I was completely caught off guard when Billy Ray called me from Nashville to ask if he could come out to visit me at the farm. I figured Jack must have granted him a type of "hall pass."

We had not seen each other for almost a month, so this visit definitely warranted a welcome home celebration. Although I was somewhat exasperated with him for neglecting me for the past few weeks, as soon as I laid eyes on him, every trace of my irritability vanished and all of those old feelings returned.

Billy Ray played me some of the new songs he had been working on and even took a few requests from me. He was excited about a "Think and Grow Rich" tape he had recently ordered. This success motivator had enraptured him and given him a new outlook on his situation. We talked about his dreams and how they were really on the way to becoming reality. It was as if time had given us the chance to reflect on everything we had been through and remember why it was we would do anything, for any chance, no matter how risky, just to be together.

Even though so much had changed even in those past few weeks, all of the feelings, all of the emotions, everything I had ever felt for Billy Ray, was just as strong despite our too-lengthy absence.

That night, we stayed awake as long as we could to savor every moment. He fell asleep in my arms. I lay awake reflecting pensively even though I was in my own bed with the man

I loved. There was some emotion that I could not quite grasp welling up inside of me. Perhaps it was an infusion of common sense. Somehow, I knew that this was the last time we would lie here listening to the spring water rumbling from the earth outside my window, snuggled up in each others' arms, letting the world outside pass us by.

Billy Ray woke up at 5:30, and I yawned, pretending that I had just woken up too, although the thoughts crashing around in my head had kept me awake all night. Billy Ray said he could not sleep any more because he felt like he needed to get out and run. I offered to throw on my sweats and run with him, anxious to see if I could run hard and fast enough to dispel the thoughts that raced around in my mind.

The morning was glorious and the mountains looked like a patchwork quilt sewn with rich golds, reds, and browns. I was huffing and puffing from having run so hard, but I managed to tell Billy Ray that I was going to the store to buy some things so I could cook him breakfast.

By the time I returned, he was in the shower, so I began preparing his breakfast. He came out clad only in a towel with his hair dripping wet. He commented that I looked good cooking in the kitchen. I knew it was intended as a compliment, so I did not take offense, although I was reminded briefly of his Chinese zodiac prediction, which warned him to "guard against being chauvinistic."

I made him a plate of fluffy scrambled eggs, sausage, hash browns, gravy, biscuits, and sliced fruit. He told me between bites that it was the best breakfast he had ever had.

While he finished getting ready, I ironed his white shirt. He looked so beautiful when he got dressed up and I told him so as I kissed him lightly on the cheek.

I walked out to the car with him and we kept trying to say good-bye. He even backed up once just to say good-bye and tell me that he loved me.

I stood in the driveway and kept waving a long time after he was gone.

———————

Chapter 29

It Ain't Over Till It's Over

Billy Ray called to see if I was going to be in town because he had a meeting with Jack and wanted to spend some time with me. He said that if I was going to be at the studio, he would stop by because he had something he wanted to give me.

I waited and waited. I knew that if Jack caught word of Billy Ray's plans about coming to see me, I would be waiting forever.

But, he finally arrived early in the afternoon. We decided to have lunch at the International Market, one of our favorite Chinese food restaurants. The restaurant was located on Belmont Boulevard, the same street as my old apartment where Billy Ray had once hung his black leather jacket and fingerless gloves. I could not help but reminisce about the other times we had driven down this same street.

When we arrived at the restaurant, Billy Ray opened the trunk of his white Beretta and showed me his new publicity photos complete with "The McFadden Agency" stamped in the lower right hand corner. The images were a stark contrast to those of the earlier Billy Ray - a man in a cowboy hat, sleeveless Jack Daniel's t-shirt, gold chains, and leather pants. The agency revamped his former macho image and dressed him impeccably in a white tuxedo shirt and pulled back his hair. He looked absolutely beautiful.

When we walked through the door, everyone dropped their plastic utensils. We went through the cafeteria-style line and had to walk in front of all the gawkers before we found a table.

I asked Billy Ray if he noticed everyone staring at him. He insisted that the people were not staring at him, but were staring at me and at my legs. We ate lunch, laughed, and talked like old times.

We rode back over to the studio and Billy Ray gave me some of his new pictures and a record he had made for distribution to disc jockeys in the area. The song on side one, "It Ain't Over Till It's Over" was produced by my father. Billy Ray proudly pointed out my Dad's name and the name of my publishing company. He asked me if I wanted to hear it and I told him we could listen to it in the studio.

Jim Allison, owner of the studio, was in the middle of a session so he told me to use the turntable in the second floor of the bedroom to listen to the single.

We walked upstairs and I put the record on the turntable as I sat down next to Billy Ray on the bed. As we listened, I told him that I really liked the remixed version. He wanted to listen to it again, so I hit the repeat button.

He asked me if he could kiss me and I did not object. He asked me if I had changed and I told him that I had not and that my feelings never would.

I don't know how many times that song played while we made love listening to "It Ain't Over Till It's Over."

Chapter 30

What a Turkey

Even with the premonition I had when Billy Ray came to see me on the farm, I still got excited to awaken to the sound of the phone ringing in the wee hours of the morning and hear the operator ask if I would accept a collect call from Billy Ray.

I saw Billy Ray so rarely during this time that I began to question our relationship. My heart and my mind waged war against one another. My mind knew that I was wasting my time, but my heart loved him so much that I could not let go.

Finally, I came to the conclusion that I needed to get on with my life. When Billy Ray made another trip to the farm to see me, I went to visit a girlfriend of mine. I knew that my best alternative now was to avoid him at all costs. I figured the toll on my heart would be a lot less if I did not have to see him.

When he arrived and discovered that I was not there, he became furious. He talked to my father, who relayed to me just how unhappy Billy Ray was. I expected him to react in this way. Billy Ray had always demanded that I accomodate to his every whim and fancy, as I always had in the past. I knew that once I stopped, he would not be happy about it.

My father then became the receiving end of all of Billy Ray's phone calls. While the lines of communication between Billy Ray and myself had been greatly altered in the last few months, his dealings with my father intensified in their frequency.

He and my father became closer in those months. In fact, Billy Ray even opened up for Dad during two shows in

Beckley, West Virginia, in February of 1990. Dad commented that Billy Ray was certainly one hard act to follow. While he waited for the smoke to clear after Billy Ray's dazzling performance, he jokingly instructed his band members, "Bring me on with "White Lightnin'" and maybe they'll think I'm George Jones!" Even back then, Billy Ray was a hard act to follow.

* * *

Billy Ray called just before Thanksgiving to tell me that he was going to be off over the holiday and wanted to spend it with me. He said that he had something he wanted to discuss with me. I wondered how he could manage to get time off from Jack and what he had to tell me, but my rational side kept telling me that I was setting myself up for a fall. Once again, I succumbed to Billy Ray's charms and forgot my vow to take charge of my life. I risked the chance that he would be here, so I declined the invitation from my sisters who were cooking the holiday dinner since our parents were in Branson, Missouri, for the holiday.

I was so excited over having Billy Ray visit that I cooked for nearly two days. I tried not to get my hopes up about what Billy Ray had to tell me, so I kept myself busy in the kitchen preparing the feast.

I painstakingly prepared turkey, mashed potatoes, green beans, cornbread dressing, broccoli and cheese casserole, biscuits, gravy, a wide variety of hors d'oeuvres, and pumpkin pie with real whipped cream.

I got a great deal of satisfaction from all my hard work and from knowing that Billy Ray would soon be with me to share the special holiday.

However, as Thanksgiving day slipped away, I grew apprehensive and restless.

Billy Ray never showed up, never did call, never mentioned it, and neither did I.

* * *

All of the hurt and humiliation that had been building inside of me for the past few months culminated in one heated conversation.

I had been poring over old magazine articles about life and love and relationships and studying "A Course In Miracles" in preparation for the speech I intended to deliver to Billy Ray.

When he called, I was prepared. I told him that I was tired of sacrificing my life for his and that it was only leading to resentment and anger. I also told him that I would no longer be coerced into feeling guilty anymore if I could not drop everything in my life to cater to his needs.

He responded that he was glad he found out now before our relationship got any further. Further? I wanted to scream at him. How much further could we get? Had we not been serious and in love for most of the past four years? I stifled my anger and let him continue on his own tirade.

He told me that I was unreasonable and stubborn. As far as business was concerned, he said that Dad and I had done virtually nothing for him. He continued his tirade by saying that we had coerced him into signing the contract with Jack, who was doing nothing for him. He said he had to do everything on his own and he was still waiting for something to happen. He was furious.

And I thought I was the one who was supposed to be angry!

Chapter 31

Billy Ray Signs With Polygram

I tried to put thoughts of Billy Ray out of my mind by keeping myself busy, but it was hard not to think of him and all that we had shared.

In an effort to keep my mind off of Billy Ray, I readily agreed to a move to Gatlinburg where I was preparing a big promotion for a Country Music Extravaganza featuring my father, Martha Carson, Ronnie Stoneman, The Good Time Charlies, many other special guests, and me. The performances would take place during the busy season at the Four Seasons Convention Center at the Ramada Inn.

Since it was nearly impossible to find a place to live in Gatlinburg, Dad and the boys in the band were forced to live in hotel rooms until they found a house near Sevierville, the home of Dolly Parton.

I would go to the house once a week to straighten up. One day while I was there with my apron on, the phone rang. I felt an electric feeling flash through my body as a voice asked for my father. I said he was in the shower. Then the voice questioned, "Kari?" and I said "Yes?" and the voice said, "This is Billy Ray."

I had not had any contact with him since the telephone episode at the farm, and although that had been some time ago, time had not necessarily healed my wounds. He tried to make pleasant conversation by asking me how I had been doing and I answered his questions with forced gaiety. I simply told him and I would have Dad call him right back when my father walked in. He asked me who was on the phone and I handed him the receiver and told him it was Billy Ray.

* * *

When Billy Ray was doing the rough demo for his album, Dad and I went by the studio to see him and Jack. I was heading back to Gatlinburg and Billy Ray made some snide comment about how I knew now what it was like to drive back and forth every week. Billy Ray and I managed to reconcile and settle our differences during this time. I finally reasoned that it took too much effort to stay mad at him, especially since he and my Dad were working so closely together. However, along with our reconciliation came the rekindling of the flame that burned between us, and that sacred candle was lit once again.

During this time, Dad was still working feverishly to help Billy Ray and I joined forces with him and did what I could do to help. Although our efforts appeared at times to go unnoticed, fate occasionally handed us a sheer stroke of luck. Dad ran into Harold Shedd, head Producer at Polygram Records, not once, but twice, at Longhorn Steaks. Longhorn, located in near proximity to Music Row, is the lunch time hot spot for all the music industry gurus. Longhorn's clientele runs the gamut from songwriting wannabes to the top executives of Music Row.

Dad talked to Harold about Billy Ray on both occasions. By this point, Dad was so encumbered in Billy Ray's career that he affectionately referred to him as "his boy." He saw in Billy Ray the chance for his legacy to be carried on and he was dead set on making it happen. He warned Harold not to let the next Elvis get away from him.

After these chance encounters, Dad went straight to Jack's office and urged him to get busy working on Harold Shedd.

Dad knew that this was Billy Ray's ticket to success.

In 1991, Harold Shedd signed Billy Ray to Polygram Records. Finally, after all the time and hard work, Billy Ray had gotten what he wanted and what he really deserved - a recording contract with a major label. But, the hard work had just begun.

In the summer of 1991, Billy Ray invited Dad and me to Millhouse Studio during the recording of *Some Gave All*. When we dropped by the studio, Billy Ray was so glad to see us. Before he sang "Someday, Somewhere, Somehow", he told my Dad that he was going in to the studio to record Dad's song. Billy Ray said he was finally going to start making some money for him for getting him to his dream.

————————

Chapter 32

McFadden Gets In My Way

Billy Ray continued to seek career advice from my father. He pleaded for Dad to call Harold Shedd to find out what the hold up was on the release of his album. During Operation Desert Storm, he called Dad begging him to get Harold Shedd to release the *Some Gave All* album.

I heard from Billy Ray again on December 19, 1991, when he called me collect, as always, and at 1:45 in the morning. He was excited because he had just bought his Mom her first CD, which was of the group Bread. I commented that our lives must still be running in sync because I had just assistant-directed a video shoot for the Remingtons, one of whom was a former member of Bread.

He told me that he had even better news. Jack had informed him today that the video company I work with was going to shoot his "Achy Breaky Heart" video and that I was hired on it. He told me that he needed me to be there to make sure it was creative in the way he wanted it. I told him that I had been waiting four years for the day to finally come. I had always dreamed I would be there and now I would! My mind reminded me that I dreamed a lot more than just being behind the scenes, but I decided not to mention it.

We then started talking about ideas for the video. He said that he wanted to shoot the video right in his own backyard with his mother with her laundry strung up and shots of the bicycles he rode for miles and miles when he was a little boy. He wanted a video that painted an accurate picture of him - rather than of some person who had grown up in a mansion.

We talked about other things we could use in the video and how our creative juices always overflowed when our minds got together.

I decided that this would be a good time to bring up the subject of his moving back to Nashville. I knew that Jack needed Billy Ray to move back because so many things were happening in his career and there was not enough time for him to commute back and forth. I had a lengthy conversation with Jack in which I presented the idea that Billy Ray could move in with me at the farm. I told Jack that it would save him money in that he would not have to pay Billy Ray's rent, but that it would also be a peaceful and familiar setting rather than an apartment in the city which might drive Billy Ray crazy.

I suppose I was being selfish because I wanted to spend as much time as possible with Billy Ray, but I *was* genuinely concerned about him. I worried about him taking care of himself.

Although I felt like I had a lot to offer Billy Ray, Jack apparently did not agree with me and had convinced Billy Ray of that, too. When I raised the subject during our conversation, Billy Ray said that he did not think it was fair for Jack to make this decision. He told me that he did not think this element of his personal life was any of Jack's business. He said he thought Jack was jealous. In the long run, however, he said that he trusted Jack and took his advice.

I was disappointed, but not surprised because I knew all along that Jack would stand in our way.

In order to hide my disappointment, I changed the subject. Billy Ray and I were deep in conversation reminiscing about our exploits in the shower at my farm house when I realized how much time had elapsed during the phone call. He said he needed to get some sleep so we said goodnight, but not before

I told him there was always a welcome mat with his name on it at my front door.

———————————

Chapter 33

The Pact

I received sporadic phone calls from Billy Ray throughout 1992. In February, he called me to give me the phone number at his apartment in Bellevue, a suburb about fifteen minutes outside of Nashville. He asked if we could have dinner soon, to which I readily agreed. Formalities over, our conversation turned to the "Achy Breaky Heart" video.

I made the mistake of making a critical comment about the video. This was merely an observation I had made. I explained that one of the most important parts of my job as Producer and Assistant Director was to watch for continuity. I explained that I was probably just overly-sensitive about this and explained that his hair was different in different parts of the video even though the performance was presented as one show. However, Billy Ray did not take my comment well. My criticism ruffled his sensitive feathers and I had to offer to take it back. It was easy to tell that despite the successes he incurred, he still had not changed a bit.

During this time, I saw Billy Ray far less often than I would have liked. He did drop by Allisongs, our studio, one day and asked me to join him at Champagne Studios where he was demoing some new songs he had written.

When we arrived, Jack was there, keeping a close watch on every move we made. He and Billy Ray were going to Gibson Guitars that day so Billy Ray could pick out his first endorsement guitar. Billy Ray said he wanted me to come along with them, and I complied. I wanted to be with Billy Ray despite the fact that Jack, along with his take-charge, overbearing tendencies, would be there, too.

As we walked out of the store, Jack asked Billy Ray what he wanted to do. Billy Ray said that all he wanted was to date me. Jack wedged himself in between the two of us and grabbed one of each of our hands. He said he wanted to make a pact with us. He looked at me with a completely possessive look in his eye and I became uncomfortable and wrenched my hand away from his stifling grasp. As I walked on ahead of him, I told him over my shoulder that I was not interested in any pact between the three of us.

Billy Ray, not sensing how serious I was, laughingly accused me of breaking a pact. He lamented that we would never know what it was Jack had to say to us.

To this day, I have no clue what the conditions of the pact might have been. I can only surmise that it might have included some restrictions on my presence in Billy Ray's life.

Chapter 34

Good Morning America

Billy Ray called me in May to invite me to the Opry House to see him perform. When I arrived, Jack McFadden immediately grabbed my hand and told me that Billy Ray was going to be so happy to see me. He then led me back into Billy Ray's crowded dressing room. Billy Ray turned around the moment I walked in, almost as if he had sensed my presence. He walked over and hugged me. I welcomed him to the Grand Ole Opry and told him how glad I was that the dreams had come true. He hugged me one more time before I left.

Billy Ray also called me before his first appearance on *Good Morning America*. He told me that he was just about to take a bubble bath in preparation for his big on-air interview. I jokingly warned him to be careful of bubble baths, reminding him of our infamous Shoney's Inn episode. I told him that the bubble bath could lead to trouble, just like it had on that faraway evening. He laughed at the memory and commented that he wished I were there to give him a back massage. We talked about the possibility of me driving to Bellevue to perform the task; however, he knew that we would be up all night. He decided we should wait for one of his days off for he had to fly to Beaumont, Texas, in the morning where the *Good Morning America* show was to be taped.

He then asked if I'd seen the headline in the newspaper that read "Elvis Lives." He was thrilled at the comparison of himself to Elvis. He also shared with me that he asked Harold to tell him over and over about the time Dad told him not to let the next Elvis get away.

He had just played a concert in D.C., and I asked him how it went and told him that I was proud of him.   Then I asked him how he was really feeling and he told me that he was just really tired.

I told him to hang in there and read him a quote from Joseph Campbell's *The Power of Myth*. The quote stated that we should always try to follow our bliss because it puts us on a path that was waiting for us all along and was the only real way to enjoy a satisfying life.

We hung up and I have not talked to Billy Ray since, but I'm happy just knowing that he really is following his bliss.

Chapter 35

It Still Ain't Over

One of the greatest elements of irony in my involvement with Billy Ray is that what brought us together may have been the very thing that tore us apart.

By 1992, Billy Ray had become a huge success. The single "Achy Breaky Heart" rocketed to the top of the charts. His album, *Some Gave All* was selling like crazy. I was extremely happy for him, although I often wished that we were still together. However, at the height of his success, I was unwillingly dragged back into his life.

The article I had written for *Entertainment Express* magazine nearly four years ago resurfaced - only this time not as a medium through which to get Billy Ray exposure in Nashville. Instead, the article served as a questionable piece of evidence regarding Billy Ray's alleged *exposure* during his days in California.

The article ballooned into the center of media attention. A huge controversy erupted over whether or not Billy Ray had been a male dancer. That story instigated a mad fury of reporters and tabloids all trying to get the facts on whether or not Billy Ray had strutted his beautiful body on stage before - perhaps less clothed than he was these days.

Naturally, I was at the center of the controversy since I had essentially broken the story. When I first heard the news, I was in Branson, Missouri, with my parents, performing in shows with my Dad. I was absolutely horrified and crushed. Billy Ray, I had been told, was denying any such involvement.

It wasn't long before the press found me. Tabloids hounded me for comment. I could not hide from all of the attention that the story had garnered.

I was shocked that everyone was making such a big deal out of the article. What I hated most was that just when Billy Ray and I had gotten back on good terms, the whole thing came crashing down around me.

Dad, Bethany, and I had been invited to his triple platinum party celebration given at BMI to honor Billy Ray for achieving sales of over 3,000,000 units for his *Some Gave All* album. He greeted me with a huge hug and would not relinquish his hold on me. He had even acknowledged Dad in his acceptance speech.

I consented to do an interview with Jeannie Williams of *USA Today*. I decided that the least I could do was try to set the story straight for Billy Ray's sake.

As if I had not been tortured enough, she asked me if Billy Ray and I had been romantically involved. This, of course, was true, but not something I was ready to make public knowledge.

When she asked if Billy Ray and I had been more than business associates, I was utterly aghast. I was not about to add to the list of controversial news swarming around Billy Ray. I answered her question by saying simply that I could understand why people might have gotten the impression that we were romantically linked because we spent so much time together. She seemed satisfied with my answer because she moved on to the real reason for the article - whether or not Billy Ray had been a male stripper.

When she asked, I decided to be evasive once again. I explained that since Billy Ray at the time of the interview was with In Concert, International, in my opinion, one of the hippest management companies in Nashville, I speculated that this story might have been some sort of promotional tool fabricated by the company so I called Scott Faragher, who said that this, indeed, was not the case. In fact, Scott told me that I could read about it in a book he had recently written called *Music City Babylon*. Despite this confirmation, I figured that I should try to take up for Billy Ray and offset this somewhat incriminating news about him.

It was months before the controversy settled down. I was relieved that all of the attention surrounding the article had died. I wrongly assumed that I could get my life back to normal.

In retrospect, I think I should have interpreted my last intimate encounter with Billy Ray as some sort of omen - making love while listening to "It Ain't Over Till It's Over" again and again. I should have understood that this was an ominous prediction for my future - because my dealings with Billy Ray surely were not over.

———————

Chapter 36

The Lawsuit

The final chapter in *My Billy Ray Cyrus Story* is, fittingly, the final chapter in my direct involvement with Billy Ray. This is perhaps the saddest part of my time with Billy Ray, and undoubtedly the most difficult to write, but nonetheless an integral element of our involvement.

When Billy Ray's status reached mega-star proportions, I felt mixed emotions. Of course I was thrilled for him. After all, he had followed his bliss and captured his dreams - what he *really* wanted all along.

But, my heart still ached from his promises. Often, I wished I had fewer visual and aural reminders of him. There was no where I could hide. He was everywhere. He was splashed across billboards. His bumping and grinding image filled my television screen. His gruff voice rang out of my stereo speakers. Being forced to bask in his incessant presence was excruciatingly painful.

My broken heart, however, was only one element of the pain Billy Ray continued to inflict on me long after our romance had faded away.

Getting over our relationship and putting my life back together was a difficult obstacle. Just when I thought I was going to be fine, Billy Ray added insult to injury: he refused to honor the terms of the agreements he had signed.

On July 24th, 1989, when Billy Ray signed the contract with Jack McFadden, we relinquished our management agreement. At that time, an agreement was arranged by my father, myself, and Jack regarding what percentage Del Reeves

Productions, Inc., would have.

As if the broken heart from which I suffered was not enough, Billy Ray escalated my hurt by his outright disrespect of my family, of me, and of everything we had done for him. It was as if he had gotten what he wanted and forgotten about my Dad, my Mom, me, and all of our hard work. He had essentially forgotten who got him where he wanted to be.

On September 23, 1992, both my Mom and Dad filed separate complaints in Davidson County Chancery Court against Billy Ray Cyrus.

My mother, who had signed an Investor Agreement at the same time Billy Ray signed the Production Agreement, filed a complaint, as well. Her complaint stated that, by contract, she was entitled to 2 1/2% of Billy Ray's gross earnings for one year after he signed a major recording label contract. She had financed two recording sessions including master tape, musicians, an engineer, studio time, background vocals, and master cassette copies of the sessions. In addition, she had paid for his hotel stays at the Country Music Hall of Fame, printing pictures, etc. - a rather extensive list. She additionally was entitled to 25% of the publishing rights on the six songs - "It Ain't Over Til It's Over," "Suddenly," "Remember," "Snooze Ya Lose," "Whiskey, Wine, and Beer," and "If Tomorrow Never Comes" - we had produced for him.

Del Reeves Productions, Inc.'s new contract for services rendered on behalf of Billy Ray had been breached, as well, according to the lawsuit. It was signed by Mom and Dad, sealed, and delivered to Jo McFadden. Jo sent the contract to Billy Ray's lawyer in Kentucky. My father called Billy Ray's lawyer numerous times for his copy of the contract, but it was never returned. We then enlisted the aid of our lawyer, Ralph S. Gordon, to retrieve our copy. However, it was not until the threat of a lawsuit that they found the signed contracts and decided not to honor the agreement.

We were left with only the alternative to sue, which we did. Billy Ray countersued on the grounds that he was misled by my father, who took advantage of him since he had no knowledge of the music business.

Interestingly enough, the contract with Del Reeves Productions, Inc., was not the first contract Billy Ray had signed. Before he became affiliated with our company, he signed a contract with Scott Faragher, which entitled Faragher to *thirty* percent of his earnings. However, Billy Ray did not sue Faragher on the basis that he was "just a man from Flatwoods, Kentucky."

The only small comfort I could find throughout the whole ordeal was the love and support that my parents gave me. We all were victims, but they understood that I had to suffer through both a broken contract and a broken heart. In order to lift my spirits, my Dad jokingly told me that he hoped I did not think he was completely oblivious to my romance with Billy Ray. He said he knew better than to think we were going out just to sit on the swing on the night of our trip to the Ragtime. My Mom said she must have been stupid because she had no inkling as to what kind of swing we had swung ourselves into!

It felt like an eternity between the initial day of proceedings until the day Ralph Gordon called to say that it was over, settled out of court. After Dad hung up the phone and told us what had happened, he, Mom, and I sat around the kitchen table and cried.

We did not cry out of relief because we no longer had to feel like villains suing America's Newest Golden Boy. Instead, we cried because of the pain in our hearts. We had taken Billy Ray's dream, made it our own, and believed in him.

Afterword

I assumed, however wrongly, that the hardest part of the end of my romance with Billy Ray would be having to get used to his not being a part of my life anymore. I have to admit that it was sometimes hard to wake up in the mornings and realize that he was not there. It was difficult not to pick up the phone and call him, although at times I longed to talk to him and hear the sound of his voice. I missed him and I missed our friendship which we vowed would last forever.

However, the shock I felt when what I thought was my one, true, perfect love died, was only one of the difficult obstacles I was forced to overcome. The swirling controversy surrounding the article I had written for *Entertainment Express* left me devastated. Similarly, the lawsuit was a veritable nightmare. When both of these horrible episodes had subsided, and just when I thought it was all over, it wasn't. Just like that fateful song had warned, "It Ain't Over 'Til It's Over." I was left, once again, to relive the past.

The August 1992 issue of *Entertainment Express* sported a full-page spread article about me, focusing primarily on my involvement with Billy Ray. I was dubbed "the mystery woman in Cyrus' past." Once people realized that I, Kari Reeves, was this "mystery woman," I had to suffer through an endless succession of questions about Billy Ray and about our relationship.

There was truly no where I could hide. Even people in my hometown of Hickman County inundated me with questions. I constantly felt eyes upon me. It seemed as though everyone was dying to get the inside scoop on Billy Ray.

I became, in a sense, a prisoner in my own hometown. Every time I ran into Hills Grocery Store, which I had frequented for years, I was bombarded with questions. The men at Fat Boys' Garage riddled me with inquiries into my personal life. Each time I tried to work out at the fitness center, the only things I could work out were my ears and my mouth - I was too busy listening to and answering questions about Billy Ray. Once the owner of The Pack Rat discovered that it was *the* Billy Ray Cyrus who had wanted to buy me that spittoon several months ago, she was extremely curious. I finally had to undergo a self-imposed exile from these places I had haunted for years. It was as if Billy Ray and his memory had driven me out of my own hometown.

This news spread throughout the music community, as well. Charlie Monk of Opryland Music Group called me one day to ask if I was the person who had brought Billy Ray to him. He said that Billy Ray had come up to him during the Country Radio Seminar and thanked him for having taken the time to meet with him. Charlie said his secretary had told him it was me and I assured him that I was indeed the person who had brought Billy Ray to him. It seems like it would have been so simple, even for a man with a Flatwoods, Kentucky, heritage to say it was me who lined up the appointment with Charlie Monk, at the time, the President of Opryland Music Group.

One day when Dad and I were at Polygram pitching another of our acts, Sandy Neese, Vice President of Communications of Polygram, came up to me, hugged me, and said "Thank you for giving us Billy Ray."

The questions have not diminished in their frequency and intensity and, to this day, people still ask me about Billy Ray. I just smile and tell them that someday, somewhere, somehow, they will be able to read about it.

It has been nearly six years since that day when Billy Ray first strolled into my office. It is certainly an understatement to say that a lot has changed since then.

Billy Ray - that nervous, aspiring country musician, from Flatwoods, Kentucky, so desperate to impress me in the interview - is now a superstar.

As for me, I never thought I would say it, but Jack was right. I was right for not making the pact. Billy Ray and I were from very different worlds. I was clouded by a dream that was never mine to start with. He now lives his dream and I live mine since the truth is no longer hanging over my head in shame, in ridicule, in silence. I continue my work in the music industry, currently owning and managing a conglomerate of music industry-related companies including Del Reeves Productions, Inc., a video production company, a publishing company, and enjoy thriving work as a producer, assistant director, production coordinator, and artist manager. I devote a large portion of my time to video production and was recently nominated for a Dove Award, one of the most prestigious Gospel music video production awards. I was also the winner of the 1993 Billboard Magazine award for Best Contemporary Christian Video for a New Artist and won best music video at the Houston International Film Festival. I am still actively involved in promoting new talent. As fate would have it, one of our artists, Chad Trout, is currently under a developmental deal with Polygram Records.

Billy Ray and I went through a lot during our times together. I watched him develop into a huge success. I helped him. I counseled him. I consoled him. I believed in him. I trusted him. But, most importantly, I loved him.

I often reflect on the Spring day when Billy Ray and I sat outside on a brick wall at the Horton Avenue Condominiums and he told me how he had once seen a Vietnam Veteran wearing a baseball cap which proudly bore the words "Some Gave All, All Gave Some." Billy Ray told me how this had inspired him to write a song about unsung heroes.

I thought the song was beautiful and I remember how touched I was when I heard its lyrics. Now, when I think about the song or hear it on the radio, I hear its words in an entirely different light.

Now, I am reminded of how much I gave Billy Ray. I gave him everything I had - I gave him my time, my help, my assistance, my mind, my heart, my body, and my soul. I loved that man so much. There was nothing I would not have done for him.

But now, after all of the pain I felt from losing him, and without even a goodbye, after the lawsuit, the controversy, and everything that followed, I look back and think that maybe - just maybe - I gave too much.

———————————